BEAUFIGHTER
at War

LONG RANGE DESTROYER.
A Beau TFX (NE343) (two
Hercules XVII, each 1,770 hp)
with full war load of cannons,
wing guns, eight 3-inch rocket
projectiles, and a 200 gallon
fuel pod slung under its belly on
the torpedo crutches./*Crown
copyright*

BEAUFIGHTER
at War

Chaz Bowyer

LONDON

IAN ALLAN LTD

First published 1976
Reprinted 1980

ISBN 0 7110 0704 7

Designed by Anthony Wirkus LSIAD

© Chaz Bowyer 1976

Published by Ian Allan Ltd, Shepperton, Surrey;
and printed by Ian Allan Printing Ltd at their works
at Coombelands in Runnymede, England

Beau X's of 235 Squadron peeling off. Nearest, EO-L is NV427.

Contents

Introduction

The history of Britain's military aviation is liberally dotted with examples of individual aircraft firms producing fine, sometimes outstanding aircraft as private ventures initially, before officialdom has expressed either interest or even encouragement in the development of the designs. Such private enterprise was responsible for splendid aircraft like the DH Mosquito and the Hawker Hurricane, to name but two examples. Another war-winner produced originally as the brainchild of an individual was the Bristol Type 156 – the mighty Beaufighter. Its conception was due simply to the inspiration of L G Frise of the Bristol company – an amalgam of ideas derived from an existing design, the Bristol Beaufort, and which in the event proved to be the most heavily armed two-seat fighter bomber in RAF operational use during 1940-45. It is also a paradox that many of the RAF's most potent aircraft, such as the sleek Spitfire and ubiquitous Mosquito, were aesthetically beautiful of line. No such praise could be applied to the Beaufighter – despite the French connotations of its name. The Beau was strictly a brutish functional air weapon – and looked every inch of it. Yet in its ugliness there was an air of pugnacity which emanated an aura of sheer rugged handsomeness; the same charisma which inexplicably attracts a beautiful woman to a boxer's battered features gave Beau crews an affinity with their steed. The pug-nosed, hunched shoulders appearance of a Beau proclaimed accurately its deadly fighting ability, a destroyer which packed the most lethal punch ever fitted to an RAF fighter at that time. A Beau's 'caress' was usually fatal – as a host of enemies came to know to their cost. Nor was this toughness limited to appearance only. The Beau was built 'like a proverbial brick out-house' (in the words of one Beau pilot), able to absorb a staggering amount of structural damage and still deliver a live crew from the debris.

The theme of this book is simple – to attempt to re-create something of the authentic 'feel' and general atmosphere of Beaufighter operations during the years 1940-45, as seen through the eyes and words of the men best qualified to do that, the Beau crews, air and ground. What this book certainly is not is a technical diatribe or 'complete' factual history of the Beaufighter; though I would hope that readers agree with my view that the accounts herein are genuine history and should be recorded for posterity before all memories fade. There is (in my view) an all-too prevalent concept that history is primarily concerned with musty files, endless tabulations and statistics, resulting in narratives indigestibly overlain with factual data extracted from

public records. Perhaps this volume will help a little in redressing the balance by paying overdue recognition of the human element in aviation history, if only in a narrow context. Despite the intimate 'she' appellation applied by its crews, an aeroplane is an inanimate complexity of fabricated technology until a human being climbs in and pushes the first button or flips the first switch.

Of the photographs used in illustration, some have been published before, but no apology is offered for re-publishing these – what may be 'old hat' to the dyed-in-the-wool researcher finds new spectators in the growing generations of aviation historians. Many have come from private collections, long-treasured photo albums and a host of individual private sources. A very large percentage of the overall total came from willing, unselfish friends, acquaintances and even complete strangers – all of whom responded magnificently to my original tentative pleas in this context. These I have listed separately, but each is owed a deep debt of gratitude.

Whilst I have tried to give a reasonably balanced panorama of Beaufighter operational facets, it should be noted that the relatively 'minor' coverage of the very early Beau night-fighting efforts is deliberate; this in deference to the several published accounts of this aspect still readily available to the avid researcher. The select bibliography provides reference to the more important past publications dealing with this (and other) Beaufighter activity.

Chaz Bowyer
Norwich, 1975

CAN OPENER. A Mk X over Sardinia making a run-in to the target for RP practice./*Imperial War Museum*

Beau X7543, the Mk VIc prototype, showing its lines to the contemporary press photographer. Engines were 1,600 hp Bristol Hercules VI, and the early straight tail planes are retained here./*Flight International*

Inspiration

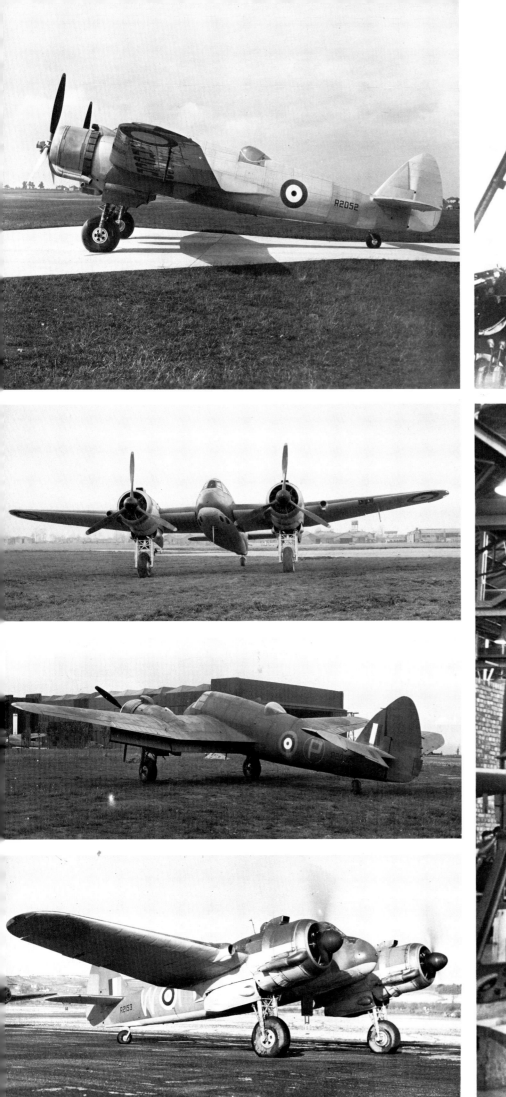

Far left, top to bottom: **FIRST OF THE LINE.** R2052 the first prototype Beaufighter Mk I, which first flew on July 17th, 1939, and was delivered to the RAF on April 2nd, 1940. Seen here at Filton, the first Beau was unarmed./*Crown copyright*

WITH TEETH. An early Mk I Beau with four 20mm cannons installed in the belly, and bullet-proof windscreen for the pilot fitted. As with all of the first 50 machines from Filton, no wing guns were yet installed./*Bristol Aeroplane Company*

R2057, a Mk 1F, incorporated slightly increased fin area, and dihedral tailplane. Used mainly as a test vehicle, it was one of two Beaus used to test the Fairey-Youngman bellows-type wing dive brakes; originally intended for nightfighter use. /*Crown copyright*

COASTAL PIONEER. R2153 (PN-W), one of the initial batch of 80 Beaus issued to Coastal Command in 1940, belonging to 252 Squadron, the first Coastal Beau unit./*Imperial War Museum*

Centre above: **THE OFFICE** – pilot's dashboard in a 143 Squadron Beau VI, a Coastal Command unit stationed at Portreath.

Above: **B-BAKER,** R2198, another of 252 Squadron's early Mk IC's, in contemporary day-fighter livery./*Imperial War Museum*

Left: **PRODUCTION LINE.** A Beau fuselage receives its mid-wing section during final assembly/*Bristol Aeroplane Company*

Night Flights

Peter Geldart came to a Beaufighter cockpit by a circuitous route. Joining the local Territorial Army artillery regiment in 1937, he went to France with the BEF at the outbreak of war. Returning to the UK in early 1940, he volunteered for aircrew duties during the Battle of Britain but did not commence pilot training until mid-1941. Originally scheduled for heavy bombers, his OTU training was changed to Blenheims and it was not until August 1943 that he achieved his private ambition to be trained for fighters, arriving at 54 OTU, Charter Hall, Berwickshire on August 4th, and posted in for training as a night fighter pilot. His subsequent service on Beaus illustrates well the cliche that war is mainly 90% boredom and 10% excitement – a continuing routine wherein the bulk of nightfighter operational flying was apparently non-productive, without glamour or glory, though not without hazards.

CHOCKS AWAY. A Canadian
pilot in the cockpit of his Beau
Mk II nightfighter gives the
ground crew a final signal,
prior to taxying out for take-off.

'On August 12th I commenced a three weeks flying conversion course onto Beaufighters by flying Beauforts, *dual* only, for which I was truly thankful. The Beaufort I with two 1,010 hp Taurus engines was a hopelessly underpowered aeroplane, incapable of maintaining a straight and level flight on one engine. However they flew these machines on operations with an 18-inch torpedo slung underneath her I shall never know – I only know I am pleased I was not asked to do it. 54 OTU was a Commonwealth unit with personnel drawn from all over the world, and it was here that I met my navigator-to-be, Pilot Officer (later, Fg Off) Howerd Kilpatrick, a taciturn member of the Newfoundland police who had left his job in Newfoundland to come over and help fight our war. His friendship was one of the nicer things that happened to me between 1939 and 1945.

The Beaufighter was as different from the Beaufort as chalk is from cheese. I found the Mk IIF fighter, with two Rolls-Royce Merlin XX, 1,280 hp engines, a real pleasure to fly. It was the first operational aeroplane over which I felt I had complete mastery. It was docile to handle, fore and aft control was very delicate and there was always a tendency to over-correct if one was ham-fisted; and whilst directional instability was ever-present, especially so during take-off and landing, if a pilot was always 'on the ball'

and ready to check swing as soon as it started he could usually stay out of trouble. Summing up, I liked the aeroplane and didn't come to any harm in her, enjoying many a pleasant flight by day and night. I think what really sold me on the Beau was the excellent, unlimited forward vision – one felt like a Chinese idol sitting right out in front of everything and yet, paradoxically, everything in front of you. The Mk VIII A.I. was a new toy to us and we were constantly sent up on practice and familiarisation, coupled with controlled interceptions where two aircraft took off within minutes of each other and take it in turns to be the 'enemy bomber' and 'friendly fighter'. Under the control of the GCI stations they would carry out mock interceptions and evasions, called in the jargon of the day 'playing with Mother'. (Another contemporary term was 'Popeye', used to convey cloud flying and visibility nil). We were fortunate to be learning our trade at the most advantageous time of the year, good weather and plenty of light at the start; while as we gained experience and proficiency so autumn, with its earlier dusks and attendant weather, was a gentle initiation to the winter months to come. Ground training was integrated with our flying training; one day we underwent ground work in the morning and flew in the afternoon, and next day this would be reversed.

Below right: **T3032, a Mk IIF, fitted with two Rolls Royce Merlin XX engines (each developing 1,280 hp) which was flown as a test vehicle for the long dorsal fin; an attempt to dampen the tendency of early Beaus to swing on take-off and landing. It also employed increased elevator area.**/*Bristol Aeroplane Company*

Below: **READY TO CLIMB IN – Flt Lt Johnson (left) and Sgt Morris of 406 ('Lynx') Squadron RCAF stand by as ground crews complete final checks on R2386, HU-M, RAF Acklington, September 15th, 1941.**/*Public Archives of Canada*

Above: **BLACK BEAUTY.**
X7873, '4' of 456 Squadron
RAAF, seen here when the unit
was based at RAF Valley,
Anglesy. Paint finish was in the
drab soot-black scheme used on
early nightfighters but later
abandoned./*R W Richardson*

Left: **MORE TEETH. R2274, A
Beau Mk V,** fitted with a 4-gun
Boulton Paul powered turret in
March 1941. In May of the same
year it was operationally tested
by 29 Squadron, and later saw
service with 406 Squadron
RCAF. A second Beau Mk III
similarly modified and test-
flown was R2306./*Bristol
Aeroplane Company*

15

We then entered the final month of our training on the Operational Flight of the OTU, away from the supervision of the main station, and were detached to the satellite airfield at RAF Winfield, about 10 miles west of Berwick-on-Tweed. Here we lived a more free and easy life, more like the operational squadrons we were later to join. Ground school was finished except for bad weather programme lectures which was very occasional – and we finally met the aeroplane we were to fly on a squadron, the Beaufighter Mk VIF, with two Bristol Hercules VI, each of 1,670 hp, plus Mk VIII airborne radar. The Mark VI Hercules engines were beautiful precision instruments and the makers' handling instructions *had* to be observed meticulously – as I found to my acute embarrassment when early on I taxied round for take-off at below minimum permitted rpm of 1,000. Half-way down the runway during take-off both my engines cut out at zero boost. The plugs had oiled up hopelessly as a result of my stupidity and I never did it again. Every plug of both engines had to be taken out, cleaned in petrol and replaced before the Beau was serviceable to fly again – I duly received a severe reprimand from my Flight commander, and some heavy sarcastic comments from the ground crew engine fitters.

The Mk VI Beau was a very different aeroplane to fly compared with the Mk II. The dihedral tailplane gave a degree of stability to the machine in all three axis, which was most reassuring. And the use of the elevator trimming tab was constantly required to lessen pilot fatigue, as is evident when one notices the placing of the tab's trimming wheel in the cockpit, close to the pilot's right hand. This feature made the aircraft a very steady gun platform. Finally our training ended and, on November 5th 1943, we left on 10 days leave prior to joining our squadrons.

I arrived at RAF Valley, on the island of Anglesey – 'Happy Valley' as it was then known by those who had the good fortune to be posted there. Commanded by Group Captain Ramsbottom-Isherwood, DFC, the station was one of the transatlantic terminal airfields, and stationed there were the USAAC, an ASR squadron of Walrus amphibians, and ourselves, 125 Squadron, with Beau VIs. We quickly settled down into the life of a nightfighter squadron – two nights 'on', two nights 'off' – and it wasn't too arduous. The weather at Valley was the best of any that could be found over the UK, and, being on the coast, 'let-down' procedure over the Irish Sea was the safest in the country.

An 'epic' flight in Beau V8751, 'D' which I was flying occurred on the night of December 28th. I was acting as target aircraft for another machine of 'A' Flight, under control of Hack Green GCI Station when at about 20,000 feet my starboard motor failed. A 'Mayday' call resulted in a homing flight over 100 miles on one engine to a master airfield at High Ercall. We made a normal single-engine approach and circuit, turning into the final approach at about 500 feet, when the port motor faltered and then also failed. The situation was depressing to say the least.

Below: **DISPERSAL SCENES. Beaus Mk II's of 456 Squadron RAAF at RAF Valley about to fly. Each aircraft bears markings of a previous unit, SA-, the identity of which has yet to be confirmed.**/*R W Richardson*

A strange airfield, black as the inside of a cow, and the realisation that I was not going to make the runway. My nav was leaning over my shoulder trying to pump the wheels back into the 'wheels up' position so that we could make a belly landing. I hadn't a clue as to what I was going to land on, so I did the only thing left for me to do, fly her as slowly and safely as possible and descend as gently as I could. Fortunately she landed in the only open space, a large field, in an otherwise built-up area. Completing a perfect 360-degrass cartwheel, the starboard wing struck first and fractured at the wing root, the port motor (white-hot by then) was catapulted 150 yards away well clear of the aircraft, and the fuselage snapped like a carrot behind the trailing edge of the wings. Fuel was pouring out of the tanks, but we both got away without a scratch!

At this time our turn came to go over to RAF Bally Halbert to do a spell with the squadron's detached Flight at this remote corner of Northern Ireland. Also at the station was a Polish Spitfire squadron, a Seafire FAA squadron from *HMS Indefatigable* and a motley collection of individuals who got on together very well in off-duty hours. Our reason for being here was that we were responsible for the night defence of Northern Ireland. Two nights after our arrival, January 25th, 1944, the local Gremlins were very active indeed. Flying Beaufighter KW117, 'M', on a GCI exercise, I had in turn my R/T go unserviceable, my 'weapon' cease to function, the port engine fail – and just as I was about to land back at the station,

the airfield lighting packed up . . . Once again, our guardian angel was 'on duty' and coped with the situation – we got down OK. The GCI calibration run to calibrate Ballinderry GCI station deserves a mention here. It was always a night exercise, carried out at heights between 10,000 and 25,000 feet. The route was to take off and fly due north under GCI control for 30 minutes then be vectored through a series of alterations of course to port every 10 minutes or so, 10 degrees at a time. This resulted in a gigantic circle being flown, the latter part of which was flown over the Irish Free State (Eire). On the night of February 5th, I was piloting KV973, 'R' on this job and soon found myself over the brilliantly – lit city of Dublin. As usual on these occasions, they greeted us with several rounds of heavy flak which burst roughly at our height but courteously clear of us. Night flying soon became less frequent, the aircraft being mainly reserved for operational scrambles; and as the Luftwaffe was not venturing out much then, our flying consisted of brief nightflying tests and nights of waiting, waiting, waiting at dispersal. It was the beginning of a restless unsatisfying time for me on 125 Squadron, and just after my return to Valley at the end of February, a call came out to nightfighter squadrons for volunteers to go onto newly-formed night intruder units of the 2nd Tactical Air Force (TAF), flying Mosquito NFs. This was the tonic I was needing, and my name went forward, and at the close of March I took my farewell of 125, Beaufighters and friends at RAF Valley.

Above: **NIGHT FIGHTER. Wing Commander D G Morris, DFC, commander of 406 Squadron RCAF at RAF Scorton, Yorkshire on July 2nd, 1942, by the nose of a successful Beau. He later rose to command of RAF Fighter Command as Air Marshal Sir Douglas Morris, KCB, CBE, DSO, DFC.**/*Public Archives of Canada*

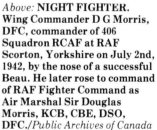

Left: **CREW ROOM CAPERS. Members of the 'Department of the Dull Rumble' staging a 'necktie party' in the dispersal hut of 409 ('Nighthawk') Squadron RCAF, Coleby Grange, Lincs., on February 10th, 1943. Personnel, left to right, are Fg Off George Bower, Plt Off Joe Cox, Fg Off John Peacock, Plt Offs Jack Bloomer, Dave Grant and Doug McBeath.**/*Public Archives of Canada*

Night Kill

John Braham ended the war as the RAF's most-decorated pilot, being awarded a triple DSO, triple DFC, AFC and several foreign decorations. He originally applied to join the RAF in December 1937, was accepted for pilot training and on August 20th 1938, at the tender age of 18, was awarded his 'wings'. In December that year he was posted to 29 Squadron at Debden – a unit with which he was to serve for nearly four years. Flying Blenheim 1F's at first, 29 Squadron helped pioneer night-fighting over England during 1940, and Braham scored his first confirmed night kill, a Heinkel III, on the night of August 24th, 1940. By the end of the year the squadron began to re-equip with Beaufighters fitted with early A.I. sets, the first to be received being R2072 on September 2nd, 1940, and the squadron flew its first operational sortie when Beau R2077 took off on the night of September 17th. Braham, known always as Bob, made his first Beaufighter night kill on the night of March 13th, 1941 – the second of his eventual credited war tally of 29 victories. His own account of this victory illustrates many of the facets

and frustrations of all the early nightfighter pilots – they were pioneering techniques which later, with experience and vastly improved technical aids, were to virtually 'clean the skies' over the UK of the Luftwaffe's bombers.

'My second confirmed success occurred on the night of March 13th, a beautiful, cold, moonlight night. Sgt Ross, my Canadian AI operator, and I were scrambled and vectored towards the coast near Skegness. As we climbed Ross was checking his radar equipment. We levelled out at 15,000 feet and with throttles wide open headed east. The GCI controller directed us towards the enemy, keeping up a running commentary. 'He's four miles dead ahead . . . you should get contact in a minute.' I asked Ross if he had picked anything up. 'Nothing yet'. Tension was mounting. On a night like this we should have seen him nearly half a mile away. To gain surprise we had to plan our approach to make it difficult for him to spot us as we came in for a kill. The controller's voice was now becoming more urgent. 'Three miles, a little to port and above' 'No contact' Then Ross came through over the intercom, 'Contact,

4,000 yards and 20 degrees above. Turn gently port.' This was it. I pressed the transmitter and shouted 'Contact' to the GCI controller. 'Good luck Bob, go in and get him.'

Now Ross had taken over the commentary where the GCI controller had left off, and was calmly directing me from the information on his scopes to a position from which I should be able to get a visual contact on the enemy. 'Where do you want him, Bob?' 'Dead ahead about 100 feet above me.' This positioning should give us the advantage. His gunners would be searching the sky, but anything coming in from below was a dark moving object against a dark background. I could tell by the tone of Ross's voice exactly how much bank he wanted me to apply as I positioned myself to close the range. 'Harder port, ease it, now steady, range 2,000 yards and he is about 200 feet above.' From these instructions I had a complete picture in my mind of the enemy's position relative to us. My eyes strained to pick up an aircraft, but not yet. We were still too far away. I adjusted the brilliance of my electric reflector sight

TAXYING NOW. A Beau VIF night fighter trundles away from dispersal./*Imperial War Museum*

Above: **ARROW-HEAD.** V8619, fitted with the early radar equipment antennae in nose and wings. This Beau saw operational service with 68 Squadron./*Crown copyright*

Right: **NIGHT 'ACE'.** Wing Commander Paul Davoud, DSO, DFC, commander of 409 ('Nighthawk') Squadron RCAF, and his dog, 'Beau', with a propeller blade from one of the unit's victims used as a scoreboard. Coleby Grange, Lincs., November 1942. /*Public Archives of Canada*

Far right, Above: **'BAMBI',** V8324 of 29 Squadron, which was taken on unit charge July 20th, 1942, but crashed on November 13th, 1942. It carried a cartoon insigne of the Walt Disney baby deer character, hence the given name/*Crown copyright*

Far right, Below: **NIGHT KILL.** The death of a Dornier 217 as seen though the nose camera of a 29 Squadron Beau on the night of October 31st, 1942 – one of three victims claimed that night by the successful team of Fg Off George Pepper and Plt Off J H Toone, DFM./*Imperial War Museum*

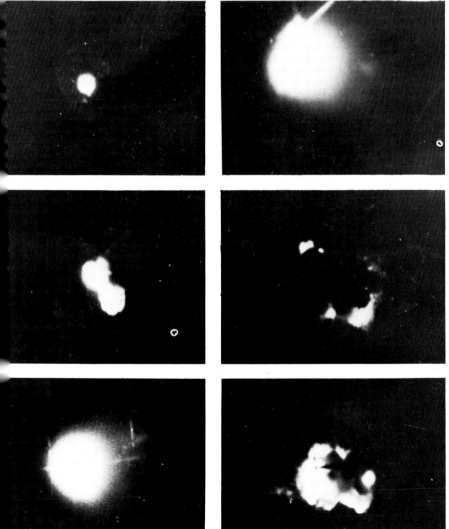

till I could only just see the reticle. If it was too bright my night vision would be impaired and it would take me longer to pick up the enemy. The range closed still further. 'Steady Bob, hold that height. He's just about 100 feet above at 1,000 yards.' 'I can't see him yet' 'OK, throttle back a bit. Range now 900 yards, hold that course.' What was that? As I stared I thought I saw something moving. I blinked. My eyes were watering with the strain. Yes, there he was, a black object moving ahead of me and above, still too far to make out what sort of aircraft he was. 'I can see him, but keep up the commentary, he's still some way off.' 'OK, 700 yards, a little to port and above.' I could now vaguely make out twin rudders. I called GCI, 'Tally-ho' I think a Dornier, will confirm when I get in closer.' 'Good show, he's all yours'.

Now I could clearly make out the enemy and identified him as a Dornier. Apparently he still hadn't seen me. I closed the range further. Ross had now taken his head out of the visor over his radar scopes and was looking ahead through his canopy in the rear of the Beaufighter. 'Can you see him yet, Ross?' After a second or two, 'Yes, I've got him now' I had to get in closer to make certain

of him. The Dornier had just crossed the coast near Skegness and might be heading for one of the Midland cities to dump his load of destruction. Now I was within about 400 yards, Ross was urging me to fire and this seemed to be the time. If I closed farther I would probably lose surprise and be spotted by the enemy rear gunners. I half expected to see tracer coming my way any minute because it was such a bright night. I eased back gently on the control column, allowing a little deflection, and pressed the firing button. The four cannons roared for a second then stopped. 'Damn it, they've jammed', I shouted. I saw a flash on the fuselage of the Dornier, where at least one of my shells had hit, and the enemy turned gently round to starboard back in the direction from which it had come. I followed. Still no return fire. I pressed the firing button again. Nothing happened. 'Oh hell, Ross, see if you can fix the guns.' Ross was already out of his seat, removing the heavy 60-round magazines from the guns and working the firing mechanism back and forth to clear the trouble. He had connected up with a radio intercom plug in the mid-section of the aircraft, as he had to leave his seat to get to the guns. 'OK, have another go, boss. I've changed the ammo drums.' I placed the gunsight again on the target. He had crossed out over the coast again, apparently hoping to head home. Still no return fire. Perhaps

I'd killed or injured the rear gunner with my first short burst. I pressed the button. Nothing happened. 'The damn things still won't fire'. 'OK, hang on. I'll try the mechanism again. I think the oil in the guns is frozen.'

I had now made up my mind that I couldn't let this aircraft get away. Perhaps we could ram it and survive. If I timed it just right and put my port wing under his starboard rudder, and then put on full right aileron quickly, maybe I could knock his tail off and he would be out of control. We were only just off our own coast and stood a fair chance of being picked up if we baled out. 'OK Ross, how are things coming along?' 'Not very good' 'Right. Get back in your seat. I'm going to try and ram him, you may have to bale out' 'Hang on a sec. Have another go with the guns. They may be all right.' One more go, and by this time the strain was beginning to tell. I didn't relish the thought of ramming the so-and-so, even though I had reasoned with myself that there was a chance of getting away with it in one piece. There was also a very good chance that we would buy it. Ross's suggestion gave me a few seconds to think.

Again I eased back on the stick and closed the range to about 50 yards as it was apparent there was no opposition from the rear gunners. The enemy didn't appear to be badly hit. There were no

signs of fire, and oddly enough he was taking no evasive action. Perhaps since I hadn't fired since the first short burst some minutes before he thought he had lost me. I pressed the button, hoping against hope that the guns would fire. The Beau bucked as they roared away and, in a blinding sheet of flame, the Dornier 17 blew up in my face. I was jubilant but poor old Ross was exhausted as he had disconnected his oxygen tube to get at the guns. Like me he was thankful that we hadn't had to ram. As we turned for home we saw the flaming wreckage crash into the sea.

The GCI operators were as bucked as we were over our success. Back at the airfield the news had gone ahead of us and we stepped out of the aircraft to be surrounded by air and ground crews. My ground crew had prepared a swastika stencil, and started to paint two of these emblems on the nose of the aeroplane before we had time to walk into dispersal hut. After we had given the 'spy' (intelligence officer) our combat report, I grabbed one armourer and asked him about the gun problem. He told me that they had been giving a lot of trouble in cold weather with oil freezing in the mechanism, which confirmed Ross's opinion. The guns in later Beaus were much more satisfactory, being adequately heated and also fitted with belt feed ammunition instead of drums.'

Beau Memories
GEORGE McLANNAHAN

NIGHT WARRIOR. An ex-604 Squadron machine (code letters NG-G are over-painted), used as a trainer on retirement from the operational scene./*Imperial War Museum*

In a wide and varied flying career, Wing Commander George McLannahan served on three Beaufighter units, 604, 96 and 153 Squadrons. This experience ran the gamut of night operations over the UK to daylight sorties in the Middle East theatre. The following fragmentary reminiscences of operating Beaufighters give glimpses of just a few of the 'routine' problems of flying the type – made all the more remarkable in his individual case by the fact that he was never 'processed' through an Operational Training Unit (OTU) before being 'thrown in at the deep end' onto operational flying.

'Having been posted (to 604 Squadron) direct from a training unit, where I'd been instructing, I never went to an OTU, and it was seldom possible to receive any dual instruction on a type – indeed, a few dual circuits on a Wellington Ic was all I ever had until I joined Transport Command in July 1943. (On joining No 264 Squadron after leaving 604, I soloed on a Mossie and a Defiant in the same morning!) My introduction to the Beau was in November 1941 with my Flight commander, Sqn Ldr S H Skinner (later killed at Dieppe observing from a destroyer) and his observer Sgt Larcey during a 45-minute night flying test. I remember John Cunningham a little later in order to reassure new arrivals on a Beau's single-engine performance used to give them a ride standing behind him in the cockpit while he cut or throttled back an engine on take-off. As a result of never having any proper instruction, and a complete lack of cockpit drills, I had many anxious moments scrambling hurriedly into the air at night wondering what I had forgotten. Fortunately however, incidents were few and far between, and the only damage I caused was a broken tail wheel caused by hard dried ruts in the mud whilst taxying at Maison Blanche, Algiers, much later. The most alarming one was an apparent ASI failure on the down-wind leg on a very dark night at Middle Wallop after selecting undercarriage down. I was pushing more and more throttle on to counteract the falling airspeed when I switched my torch on for a quick look round the cockpit. I found the undercarriage was still up but we had full flap down!

Another incident I'll not forget was after a night flying test at altitude. I'd dropped in to pick up someone and found after switching off on the tarmac that I'd not pushed the undercart selector fully down, and the locking bolt (operated by the aircraft weight on the undercarriage) was underneath instead of through the ring under the selector lever. This was not all, however. On taking off again towards Harrow-on-the-Hill from Northolt, despite bags of indicated power, there was a marked reluctance to depart from roof-top level. This was cured by moving the supercharge selector back to 'M' instead of the 'S' position it had been left in before starting our descent into Northolt. The most frustrating incident was during one of the few operational, as opposed to practice, chases when our port engine failed way out over the Channel heading south or south-east. Realising I had run dry on one tank, and that the starboard engine would shortly follow suit, I changed over both fuel cocks by reaching behind me with my left arm. The port engine did not restart and we reluctantly gave up the chase to return to base. On checking further with that essential and

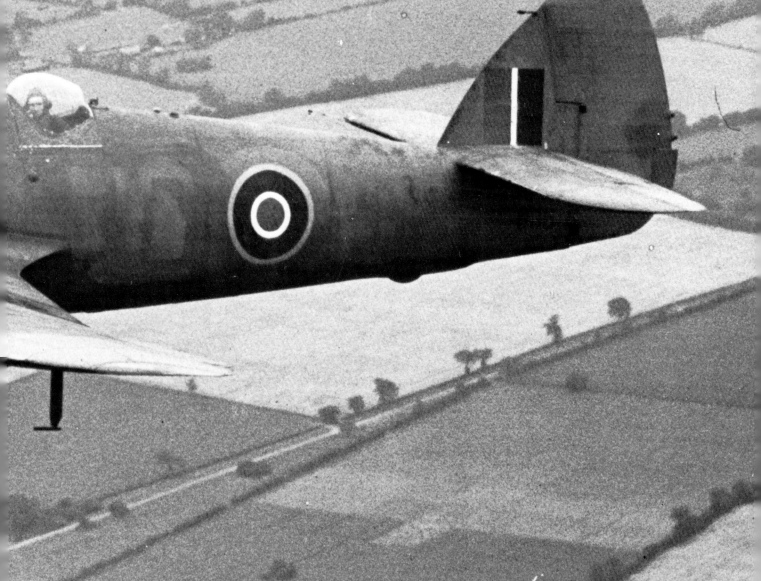

useful torch I found that in my hurry I'd turned the port cock twice to 'Off – and the starboard was still on its original tank. We then got the port engine restarted but too late. I don't recall much engine or airframe unserviceability, but much AI trouble, often in 'smoke and smell', and quite a bit of R/T trouble – mainly weak TX or reception. We only carried one four-channel VHF set (as far as memory serves me). The ground staff certainly did a fine job in maintaining our aircraft and engines in all the squadrons in which I served, and this was often if not usually carried out in the open, in all weathers. I see from my log book that in the three Beau squadrons I only did 315 hours flying, and less than half of that at night. A good month's total on an NF unit was about 50 hours. A particular memory of 604 Squadron was of a certain young Pilot Officer who was a good pilot in many ways but was christened 'Prune' by the squadron. I was returning from a patrol in another Beau and heard him overshoot and say he was on one engine. He was missing when I joined the circuit but I got permission to investigate a fire on the ground that I could see to the south. I could recognise the tail of a Beau sticking out of the bonfire during a low pass. His observer pulled him out of the wreck. The pilot had a broken thigh and was reputed to have told the MO in the ambulance that he he'd be OK as he was 'only doing 110 mph when he hit'! The dear boy had forgotten to change over his fuel cocks after being up for about four hours.

Memories of 153 Squadron in North

Africa are few and mainly non-operational. Such as taking AVM H P Lloyd (our AOC) to Aboukir and Heliopolis and back for a conference. It was supposed to have been a night flight there and back, but I applied the time difference incorrectly eastbound and it was well after dawn when we reached Aboukir. The return flight which took nine hours and 20 minutes (20 minutes longer than the flight east) is memorable for a lack of navigation aids. There were some beacons whose characteristics changed nightly. And when I went into Heliopolis Operations Room the night of the return trip the Americans who were there couldn't find the codes for that night – the previous duty officer still had them, or the key to their container and he was off duty! We got Tobruk to give us a visual fix on a cone of searchlights and a few VHF bearings from Benina. Castel Benito, Tripoli, eventually homed us in on VHF 45 minutes late on ETA. I'd had some anxious moments until we eventually established radio contact with them, wondering what a night forced landing in the desert with the AOC aboard would do for me. We refuelled at Castel Benito both ways, incidentally. On arriving back at Maison Blanche at dawn I remember the AOC asked me how I felt, and I said 'Fine, thank you' – but after breakfast in the Mess I slept soundly for nigh on 24 hours . . .

On June 5th, 1943 my observer, Flt Sgt Lancashire, and I went on an ASR search and located two members of a Hudson which had ditched. What a small and difficult target a dinghy is to find and keep in sight until one is relieved. The Mediterranean was a rude awakening weather-wise. One fondly imagined on arrival that one was coming to an area of fine weather, but in January 1943 we found ourselves operating in far worse conditions than in the UK, and with far fewer aids to navigation. It didn't really clear up until May and even then we had the odd diversion due to fog at base. One such to Orleansville was memorable. The airfield had highish ground around it so I took particular care to stay 'in the green' of the GPI all the way down. Imagine my thoughts when on taxying back to the threshold to leave the runway I found that the American-type runway merely had green threshold lights.

As for the Beaufighter as an aircraft, I found the Mk I a strong and powerful machine but very tiring to fly on patrol at night, or on instruments, as it was completely unstable fore and aft. This was virtually cured on the Mk VI. I came onto the Mk VI after flying Mosquitos and it was like handling a battleship after being used to a destroyer. On this aspect I'll always remember an American in 153 Squadron who had joined the RCAF early on to get into the war. He commented that he felt completely at home in a Beau as he'd previously been a truck driver! Rather unfair on the Beau as it was a very fine, solid aircraft. For just one example of this, landing it in a cross-wind was never a problem; once placed properly on the ground it sat there and defied any deviations.

Top left: **V.I.P. Beau. Beaufighter VIF of 307 (Polish) Squadron arriving at the squadron's base at Exeter, September 1942, bringing the C-in-C Polish Forces, General Sikorski on an official visit.** */J B Cynk*

Centre left: **FIGHTING TEAM. Sqn Ldr George McLannahan (rt) and Flt Lt R C ('Bob') Wright, in front of Beau I, T4637, NG-O, 604 Squadron. Wright later wrote the definitive biography of his ex-'Chief' Sir Hugh Dowding.** */Wg Cdr G McLannahan*

Bottom left: **ALL SET TO GO. Sqn Ldr George McLannahan in his 'office' prior to a patrol, 604 Squadron, RAF Middle Wallop.** */Wg Cdr G McLannahan*

Above: **All the comforts of home . . . Some of 604 Squadron's crews outside the Pheasant Hotel (Andover-Salisbury road), 1942, when it was used as the unit's officers' Mess. Identified personnel here include (l-r), Unknown; Unknown; Foster; Rod Bugge (Norwegian); Norwegian pilot; Hoy; Maxwell; Wg Cdr John Cunningham, DSO, DFC; Flt Lt Bob Wright; and Plt Off Jimmy Rawnsley, DFC, DFM.** */Wg Cdr G McLannahan*

From Ground Level

FRED PEDGEON

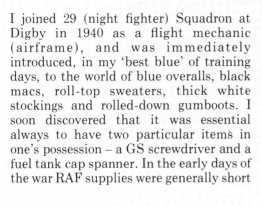

I joined 29 (night fighter) Squadron at Digby in 1940 as a flight mechanic (airframe), and was immediately introduced, in my 'best blue' of training days, to the world of blue overalls, black macs, roll-top sweaters, thick white stockings and rolled-down gumboots. I soon discovered that it was essential always to have two particular items in one's possession – a GS screwdriver and a fuel tank cap spanner. In the early days of the war RAF supplies were generally short – for example, gumboots. Often it happened that on leaving our muddy satellite 'drome at Wellingore our gumboots would be retained for the night crews just coming on duty. If you had no pre-warning of this arrangement, and did not have your gumboots with you, it was quite a sight for the Station Warrant Officer (SWO) and the guardroom to see a Bedford truck disgorge its load of boot-less airmen, with the few who were shod piggy-backing the unlucky ones over rain-soaked paths back to their billets!

For a short while I worked on very dilapidated short-nosed Blenheims until the day in September 1940 when our first Beaufighter arrived. This was received with quite a sense of awe and wonder because of their great size and the two huge Hercules engines. As they arrived in quantity the new aircraft were allocated round the squadron, but the air and ground crew who operated the first of these new kites were regarded as the 'gen

BURMA TABLEAU. Ground crews start refurbishing a Beaufighter which belly-landed./*Imperial War Museum*

Above left: **REPAIR GANG.** This Beau, its hydraulics ruptured by Japanese groundfire, force-landed on a river bank near base on return. Nothing daunted, the 'erks' prepare to get it back into operation state./*Imperial War Museum*

Centre left: **OVER-MANNED.** An over-posed view purporting to show 'armours re-arming a Beaufighter', in this case V8748, ZJ-R of 96 Squadron at Drem, Scotland, in October 1943. In the foreground two armourers are 'pulling-through' a 20mm Hispano cannon; while behind them no less than seven WAAFs load cannon shell boxes. In practice, two men was normally the maximum complement of armourers available for such a task . . ./*Imperial War Museum*

Above right: **LIBYAN SCENE.** A 252 Squadron Beau undergoing a major inspection among the palm trees and desert backdrop./*British Official photo*

Centre right: **ROYAL THANKS.** Ground staff of 455 Squadron RAAF receive a personal 'thank you' for their sterling work from Air Marshal, HRH the Duke of Gloucester./*R.A.A.F. Official*

Bottom left: The close 'involvement' felt by most operational units' ground staff with their machines and air crews is part-exemplified here by the keen interest displayed by the erks of 404 ('Buffalo') Squadron RCAF in flak damage to the fuselage of Fg Off A B French's Beau, EE-B, at Davidstow Moor, Cornwall, August 21st, 1941./*Public Archives of Canada*

Bottom right: **FROM THE M.U.** A new Hercules engine is inspected by maintenance crews of 406 ('Lynx') Squadron RCAF at RAF Valley, April 22nd, 1943. L-R: Sgt N R Cuthbert; LAC D Gibson; Cpl H G Robertson and LAC A B Gibb./*Public Archives of Canada*

kiddies' of the squadron. There was a lot to learn, and the habit of two riggers jack-knifing themselves over the tail of a Beau during engine run-up (as previously done on Blenheims) was soon abandoned before those poor unfortunates were blown off their feet by a howling slipstream. The early Beau had large drum ammunition for the four cannons, items which were none too popular with the AI operator in the rear fuselage, who had to re-arm with the heavy drums in poor light whilst in flight. Ground crews too found the four drums locked across the fuselage floor a hazard, and the cause of many cut and bruised ankles. Engine priming had to be carefully watched – if there was a little too much, either the engine would fail to fire or a sheet of flame would shoot out of the exhaust. The Beau was possibly the first such aircraft fitted with entry and exit escape hatches. When released for emergency in the air they caught the airstream, swung open, locked tight, and gave a clear drop for the pilot and his operator into space.

The early radar sets brought their teething troubles, with calls that 'M-Mother' was returning with a 'bent weapon'. Tail wheel troubles soon developed, with a nasty shimmying on landing, but eventually most snags were solved with new and better components, and the Beau settled down. One serious fault was stern frame cracks which occurred after a series of moderate landings. Engineers from the Bristol company stayed with the squadron for many months, modifying and strengthening the stern frame. The overall black paintwork was also changed several times, ranging from a dull black which was slightly shiny, to a final sooty non-reflective black. Air crews were supplied with a tube placed near their seats to answer nature's call on the cold winter nights, and occasionally a rather embarrassed pilot would return saying, 'I've used the P-tube, laddie', and the rigger would have the job of flushing it out. One other minor snag concerned the air bottles on pilot dinghies which tended to inflate prematurely whilst the aircraft was in flight. This fault resulted in at least one fatal accident, and pilots later carried knives in their flying boots to puncture the dinghy should this occur.

In 1941 came a welcome move to West Malling in Kent – Lincolnshire was not much loved – and we exchanged the view of potato fields and sugar beet for the blossom of fruit orchards. Business picked up too, being stationed south of London, and 29 Squadron had its fair

31

share of 'bandits' in the area. All this has been well recorded in Guy Gibson's book *Enemy Coast Ahead,* and Bob Braham's *Scramble,* but perhaps a personal mention should be made of those two famous pilots. Guy Gibson came off a tour with 83 Squadron, Bomber Command. flying Hampdens, and during his time with 29 got three enemy aircraft. I well remember him for his sense of fair play and total dedication to flying; though incidents like taking off full-bore at night from dispersal, just clearing the boundary trees in his efforts to get a Hun were also very memorable. One day Guy decided to air-test the Beau I was servicing and, naturally, was accompanied by his AI operator. Unfortunately the Beau had previously been operating on test with no operator in the rear, and to counter-act this loss of weight, heavy lead ballast weights had been installed. Guy sat in the cockpit with engines running, chafing at the bit, whilst the rigger and engine mech sweated blood getting 20 heavy lead discs off an upright rod bolted to the bulkhead as quickly as possible. Bob Braham was a fun-loving personality, a man who would happily muck in and help in all sorts of ways. At Wellingore, near Digby, he would help refuel his aircraft when it was dispersed from the main parking area before taxying back to the main site. Two other well-known personalities on 29 were Graham Little and George Pepper. Graham Little would always call Guy Gibson's famous dog Nigger, a 'black bastard'. George Pepper, with his close-cropped hair, was well liked, despite his quiet manner. He was a Canadian and a former TT rider at West Ham. Both men were later killed – Graham Little flying a Mosquito, and George Pepper in a Beaufighter on air test over Crowborough. My own pilot was C V Winn, who possibly flew the first Beau with a 'shark-mouth' nose.

As an airframe flight mechanic I felt very much part of a team, comprising the air crew and three flight mechanics. Though we recognised the importance of the other vital trades, such as armourers and fitters, we did not consider them to be actually part of *the* ground crew, as we were. The engine mech serviced and ran the engines, tested for mag drops etc. The airframe mechs serviced all hydraulic and pneumatic systems, checked aircraft controls, and carried out undercarriage retraction tests. All three refuelled, locked and covered the aircraft against bad weather. They 'scrambled' with the aircrew, secured them in their seats, often

Above: **NASAL SURGERY. LAC R L Trusty inspecting the innards of Beau's nose, 406 Sqn RCAF, RAF Valley, April 22nd 1943. The unit's Canadian associations are displayed by the maple leaf insigne painted on the side.**/*Public Archives of Canada*

Left: **ENGINE MECH. LAC O E Barker servicing a Beau's port engine, 404 Squadron RCAF, RAF Tain, Scotland, July 29th 1943. Noteworthy are the 'flame-damper' exhaust extensions fitted here.**/*Public Archives of Canada*

Above right: **Maintenance complete and aircraft declared operational, the air crews arrive at dispersal to take over. (L-R); Flt Lt F W Hillcock; Sgt E K Vickers; Fg Off H J Findlay; Sgt M M Vineberg; and Flt Lt D D Carr-Harris leaving the 'paddy-wagon', 406 Sqn RCAF, RAF Acklington, September 15th, 1941.**/*Public Archives of Canada*

started the engines beforehand etc. They saw the aircraft in and out of dispersal, and worried about the aircrew and 'their' aircraft's return. And when the aircraft did return, they fought to get the engine bowser first. There were huge, heavy asbestos covers which had to be wrapped around the Beau's engines and heaters to be placed underneath – the English winters during the war were really something ... Of course just caring for the engines was not sufficient; the cockpit and rear cupola required covers, plus interior heaters to protect instruments against condensation, not forgetting the precious radar sets. it was often quite a game on a winter's night, lighting the internal heaters in an underground dispersal shelter and then staggering out into an icy, howling wind – only to have the flame blow out again and again.

One of the more onerous features of servicing the Beau was spreading anti-

icing paste on the leading edge of the main-plane to prevent icing up in the air. This consisted of a toffee-like substance which had to be rolled, stretched and stuck on as best as frozen hands would allow. It was found that a wad of this stuff boiled up in a discarded four-gallon petrol can helped to melt it somewhat. (The fire was provided by another four-gallon petrol tin filled with sand and petrol and ignited.) Another discovery was that the Beau exhausts were so hot that they glowed at night, so a pink distemper-like paste was used to minimise the tell-tale glow. The daily life of the squadron followed a pattern of inspections in the morning, air tests in the afternoon, and operational flying after dusk. At a place like West Malling (a permanent station) life was busy but fairly comfortable. At a satellite 'drome, with the odd hut and hangar and thick mud, with no facilities, things could be very uncomfortable indeed.

West Malling had its share of bombing in 1940, with the result that only the ground floors of the barrack blocks were occupied. Half the ground crews were stationed in the camp, but (for fear of bombing) the other half were billetted at a country house near Tonbridge, a house with tennis courts and a fish pond. All ground crews here had bicycles, and cycling to the 'drome on an early spring morning through the orchards and hop fields was a pure joy. Another pleasurable memory was the early evening before flying commenced, with air and ground crews quietly sitting outside the crew huts or doing small jobs in preparation for the coming night's work. The air crews would read, talk, check their kit; while the ground crews would have parachute and

seat straps laid out ready for their particular air crew. Windscreens would receive a final polish, trolley accumulators would be humming away, while in the far background the odd tractor (farm or RAF) could be heard. Flying sometimes came quietly, sometimes on 'scramble'. While awaiting the Beaus' return the ground crews would have a hot supper delivered to dispersal – meat, potatoes, veg, with cheese, bread and cocoa to last the night. When the kites came back, and the 'erks' scrambled up ladders and on main-planes, they often wished they'd had smaller suppers – indigestion was common! After the stand-down at dawn, with maybe a Hun or two 'collected' during the night, there was a rush back to billets for a hot bath and sleep. Despite the cold, skinned knuckles and the mud, servicing the Beau did in all honesty give us some sense of purpose, and the feeling of a job well done.

Above: **ERKS. An informal group of ground crews of 406 Sqn, RCAF at Predannack, Cornwall, January 25th, 1943, in front of Beau HU-V. Front row, L-R: LAC J W Buck; Cpl F E Fisher; Flt Sgt 'Chiefy' J Tumilty; LAC C Marier. Rear row, L-R: Cpls W Johnston; D A Walker; LACs S Rigel; J A Draze, & Cpl E F McCarl.** */Public Archives of Canada*

Desert Beaus

REV-UP. One of 272
Squadron's early Beaus at
Edcu, September 1941.
Noteworthy are the oil-
spattered nose and sand-
encrusted main wheels./*British
Official photo*

Above: **272 Squadron's erks pause to watch (and, no doubt, criticize . . .) another of the unit's Beaus doing a low-level beat-up of the airfield at Edcu, near Alexandria. Flying Beau can just be seen under 'K's' starboard wing.**/*via D Vincent*

No 272 Squadron introduced the Beaufighter to the Middle East theatre of operations, having exchanged its former Blenheims for Beaus at Chivenor in April 1941, and flying to Alexandria, Egypt in the following month. From then until the squadron's final disbandment on April 30th, 1945, the unit's Beaus fought throughout the North African campaigns, went to Malta, Sicily and Italy. Their duties, like a majority of Desert Air Force units, were multitudinous – anti-shipping strikes, bomber escort cover, and especially the exhilarating (from a pure flying and close 'involvement' viewpoint) task of low level strafing of enemy transport and installations. The variety of exploits undertaken by 272 Squadron have been well described in Victor Houart's book, *Desert Squadron* (Souvenir Press Ltd, London, 1959). The following reminiscences are those of Wing Commander C.V. Ogden DFC, who commanded 272 at Edcu (Idku), near Alexandria during its early operations along the North African coast and across the Mediterranean.

'My first experience with the Beau was as a test pilot with the Bristol Aeroplane Company at Filton, where I played a small part in its development and carried out many production flight tests. During early 1941, however, I felt that as I had spent so many years training to be an operational pilot I just had to have a 'go' and, as several Blenheim squadrons were being converted to Beaus at about that time, the Air Ministry rather welcomed my return, and I was posted to 236 Squadron at Carew Cheriton, South Wales in the summer of 1941. The main

function of this squadron was to act as long range fighters covering the Western Approaches between southern Ireland and the Bay of Biscay. This proved to be a very dull occupation, however important it might have been, but it meant a great deal of flying in all weathers over a distinctly unfriendly ocean. It was only the very lucky pilots who ran into a long range Focke Wulf 'Condor'. In the autumn of 1941 the squadron was disbanded and the crews were all posted to the Middle East, flying our aircraft via Gibraltar and Malta to Cairo. The flight to Gib was uneventful, although the 900 yard runway (as it was then), coupled with extreme turbulence caused by the Rock, was a bit worrying to many pilots. The next leg to Malta was through very bad weather as far as Tunis. When we arrived at Malta a bombing raid was in full swing but owing to our shortage of fuel we had to land while the bombs were still dropping. Further raids during the night slightly damaged my Beau but not sufficiently to hold me up, and next morning we took off during a raid. Messerschmitt 109s were waiting for us as we left the island and four of our eight aircraft were lost. The rest of the flight was tiring but uneventful.

There were two 'Coastal Beau' squadrons at this time in the Middle East, 272 and 252, both located at Edcu, close to Alexandria, and the newcomers were divided between them with me going to 272 Squadron. Our Beaus carried out various functions; first as long range cover to shipping in the Mediterranean, with an emphasis on protecting convoys to Tobruk and Malta. We also flew anti-submarine patrols over all Royal Navy

Above: **DESERT SCOURGE. A 272 Squadron Beau at 'zero' feet over Edcu airfield, Egypt, September 1941 – normal operational height for the unit's road-strafing operations, along the Libyan coast road during 1942.**/*Imperial War Museum*

ship movements. Some of these sorties were dull and routine, but when the convoys were attacked, all hell broke loose, and on one Malta convoy eight Beaus were lost with only one of the crews being picked up. I can recall one particular sortie vividly when we were briefed to give cover to the Fleet returning from a commando raid on Tobruk. I was to pick them up at first light when they were returning to base, but when I eventually located them, one cruiser and five destroyers, they were heading back towards Tobruk. This was more surprising because there was cloud cover of five-eighths at 3,000 feet and, as the Fleet was expecting a torpedo attack, we had been ordered to give low level cover. When the attack came it was by wave after wave of dive bombers coming straight through the clouds. I took my Flight up through the clouds to intercept but their numbers were too great to cope with. Although we felt sure we'd downed some of the attacking aircraft, these were impossible to confirm. In the meantime it was obvious that most of the ships were damaged, and the cruiser had received a stick of bombs right along its deck from a Ju 88, and was obviously finished. When its crew had been rescued, the cruiser was eventually sunk by one of our destroyers. Hours later the three surviving destroyers limped into Alexandria.

We often gave top cover to torpedo bombers and on one occasion, with four Beaufighters, gave cover to a squadron of Beauforts on a shipping strike in the vicinity of Malta. This was a long, tedious flight as we had to cut our speed considerably to stay with the Beauforts. We had been briefed to pick up the bombers in the Alexandria area and cover them to the target, and when they made their attack we were to take on any German fighters and create a diversion. After the attack on the target ship it was then every man for himself and to make for Malta (who had agreed to send out fighters to bring the Beauforts home). About eight miles from the German convoy two Me 110s flew over us, 500 feet higher, but we were 'on the water' and they apparently didn't see us. However, Wing Commander W. Riley (one of the truly great characters of the war) who was immediately below them, could not resist the temptation. He pulled up his nose, and in two short bursts brought both of them down – wonderful marksmanship. Of course, the convoy was immediately alerted and a few minutes later we flew into a great reception. Greatly outnumbered by Me 110s and Ju 88s, we managed to keep them off the Beauforts, and when the last torpedo had been dropped we broke off and headed for Malta. At that stage two Hurricanes passed us to bring in the Beauforts – apparently this was the maximum number of fighters that Malta could produce! All our Beaufighters made base, but we learned later that some 50 Me 109s had joined the fray and the Beauforts took a severe beating. I seem to recollect that only five made it, and even they were still being attacked by 109s when they entered the circuit at Luqa. This was just one of several similar operations.

I personally think the Beaufighter did its best work on ground-strafing missions. Various types of target were attacked, but I always felt that the best results were obtained on road-strafes. Hundreds of

Above and left: **Two views of Beau T3316, 'M' of 272 Squadron, 1941. It carried the soubriquet *'PEGASUS'* on the port side of the nose.**/*Imperial War Museum*

Above right: **DESERT KINGS. Personnel of 272 Squadron lined up for inspection by HRH Duke of Gloucester, early 1942. From left: Plt Off Deppe (Belgian Air Force); Plt Off Hodgson (RCAF); Plt Off Pete Cobley, DFC, (RAF); Fg Off Delcour (Belgian Air Force); HRH; Wg Cdr C V Ogden, DFC (OC Sqn); and staff officers.** /*Wg Cdr C V Ogden, DFC*

Right: **BEAU 'ACE'. Squadron Leader Anthony A Watson, DSO, DFC, who served with 272 Squadron at one period, then commanded 227 Squadron before his death in action. His war tally was at least 12 victories.**/*Imperial War Museum*

enemy transports were destroyed or damaged by the Beaus. Our usual technique was to send out two sections, fly about 15 miles out to sea, then turn west parallel to the coast until opposite the target area and then turn in. Having approached well below any radar cover, we preserved an element of surprise. As we approached the road one section would turn right and the other went to the left. With No.2 about a mile behind the leader, we would then fly down the road at zero feet and fly straight at vehicles on the road. A quick burst at 100 to 50 yards, pull up over the roof of it and down on the road again, ready for the next. Any vehicle missed by the leader would be finished off by his No.2, and if we ran into a convoy there were plenty of pickings for a No.2. Only on two occasions did aircraft actually scrape the road with their airscrew tips, but in each case the Beau returned safely.

The Beau had an operational range of over 1200 miles so we were able to attack targets up to 600 miles behind the enemy forward positions. I recall one long range attack when the battle lines were in the

Above: **BEAU LEADER. Wing Commander George Hedley Stainforth, AFC, an ex-Schneider Trophy team member, who commanded 89 Squadron in 1941/1942, and was killed in action flying Beau X7700 on the night of September 27/28th, 1942.** */MOD(Air)*

out three more attacks from differing directions and although I could see considerable damage to the lorry and its contents, the brute just wouldn't catch fire. So I left it and flew down the road. No other targets appeared and at El Agheila I turned left and headed for base – total flying time for this sortie being six and a half hours.

Another function often allocated to Beaus was aerodrome strafing – *very* unpopular with Beau pilots. Enemy airfields were always very heavily defended with light flak and the gun crews were always on the alert. I remember one such attack during the Allied retreat to Alamein, when we were briefed to strafe LGs 05 and 121 at Sidi Barrani with five Beaus. Using our normal technique we crossed the coast at zero feet and as we approached the coast road we saw it was choked with enemy traffic. We each put in a good burst in passing without breaking formation. Landing Ground 05 appeared within a minute so we pulled up to 500 feet in line abreast and dived to attack. The cupboard was bare – no targets and no opposition. So on to LG121 and at one mile we again rose to 500 feet and dived to attack. They were certainly ready for us and the sky was filled with bursting flak and tracers. The only visible targets were three lorries well out into the airfield, surrounded with Jerricans. They were obviously flying in petrol in Junkers 52s to keep the forward panzers going. We attacked and could see petrol cans being hurled in every direction, but again, no fires. Obviously we were too late and what we'd strafed was a dump of the 'empties'. It was then every man for himself and, flying at zero feet again, we headed out to the coast. I then noticed an open lorry coming from the coast and filled with personnel. I turned and attacked, with devastating effect, and as I pulled away over the lorry I noticed their undressed appearance and a number with towels around their necks. I realised that it must have been a bathing lorry returning from the coast, and it left a nasty taste in my mouth.

During the desert campaigns the Germans often brought in supplies and reinforcements by air, the aircraft usually used being Junkers 52s which flew from Crete to the Tobruk area. These were usually in formations of up to 20 aircraft, flying at deck level, and we were often sent out to intercept, but it was always difficult to make contact. However, on one occasion when we were on an armed recce between Mersa Matruh and Tobruk

Gazala area. I took off from LG 121 (Sidi Barrani) at 0300 hours and headed straight for El Agheila across some pretty rugged territory. I found it very dicey trying to maintain an altitude of 50 feet in pitch darkness. However, I arrived in the target area at first light and my first 'juicy' target was a staging post on the road where a small convoy of six vehicles had obviously pulled in for breakfast. I started with a burst from all four cannons and six machine guns through the roof of the canteen, and immediately there were Germans running in every direction and diving for cover. I then made three attacks on the vehicles, severely damaging them, but was disappointed that none of them caught fire. I next flew to the coast where a small supply boat was unloading at a jetty, and made two passes with obviously good results. I then flew across the bay of Syrte and rejoined the coast road about 50 miles south of Benghazi, proceeding south in search of more transports. It was very quiet on the road but eventually a heavily-loaded ten-ton truck appeared going north, and I took him head-on. The driver saw me coming and attempted to pull up, but when I fired I shattered his windscreen and saw him collapse on his seat. I carried

we sighted about 20 Ju52s in tight formation right on the water and about 20 miles out from the coast. As previously arranged, I ordered five Beaus to climb and act as top cover, and the other five to follow me, long line-astern, and we made a head-on attack. I hit the leader in my first attack and saw him going down – later in the battle I saw him in the sea. Coming round to the front to make my second attack, I could see I was hitting him but he still failed to go down. As I pulled over the top of him I was surprised to see that some of the fuselage windows were open and 'Tommy' gunners were having a go at us. As I came in for a third attack I suddenly saw the sea being churned up underneath the nose of my Beau. When I asked my navigator if there was anything on my tail, he calmly informed me that an Me 110 was about to make *another* attack! With his superior manoeuvrability and speed I just couldn't shake him off. I was 'sniping' over the sea for a good five minutes, with the 110 knocking hell out of me, before I spotted another Beau and turned towards him; whereupon the Messerschmitt broke off the fight. I limped home to make a dicey landing with a burst tyre and 73 bullet holes in the fuselage. A disappointing

sortie as, although we had damaged several Ju's, we could only claim two as definitely destroyed.

Yet another task allocated to our Beaus during the desert battles was attacking small supply boats (F-boats) which were used in large numbers to carry supplies to enemy advance formations along the coast road. They were usually in convoys of six to eight, and always had fighter protection. This was, again, an unpopular target with the Beau crews as the boats always had a single-engined fighter cover, and the boats themselves were heavily armed, each having one 88mm heavy flak and four light anti-aircraft guns. For these attacks I had our Beaus fitted with two rearward-firing Lewis guns, one in each engine nacelle, plus an additional free Lewis gun for the navigator. All three guns were loaded entirely with incendiary bullets; the idea being that when enemy fighters came in to attack we filled the sky behind us with a good pyrotechnic display, which caused the enemy fighters to hesitate just long enough for us to make our own attack. Then down on the water and away. We were quite successful in these attacks, and in 1942 over 100 boats were credited as sunk by 272 and 252 Squadrons.

Above: **SCOREBOARD. 89 Squadron crews and the wing cross taken from the unit's first victim which was then used as 89's 'Tally Sheet'. Standing, fifth from left, is the squadron commander, Wg Cdr G H Stainforth, AFC.**/*Gp Capt K W T Pugh, AFC*

Above: **Flying Officer H H K Gunnis, DFC, a 5-victory Beau pilot in 252 Squadron 1941/42. 252 Sqn received its first Beau, T3328, on March 8th, 1941.** */Imperial War Museum*

Right: **FLAK VICTIM. A 252 Squadron crew on a road-strafe in December 1942 were hit by ground fire and forced down in the desert. A passenger snapped the pilot (rt) and observer by their Beau before they set out to walk back to base – a trek of several days and nights before they were retrieved by a British armoured car patrol.**

Above centre: **Flying Officer N D Cox of 39 Squadron, who shot down four Junkers 52's in two days as the Afrika Korps evacuated Bardia. He was subsequently shot down by Messerschmitt Bf 109's over Sardinia, but evaded capture and rejoined his unit later.** */Imperial War Museum*

Far right, top: **BEAU TEAM – air and ground crews pose in front of their 39 Squadron aircraft, Algehero, Sardinia, 1944.** */T C Hellier*

Sumburgh to Malta

H J GARLICK

ROCKET STRIKE. On August 8th, 1944, escorted by Mustangs of the 8th Air Force, USAF, a Coastal Command strike force of Beaus attacked a convoy of 12 enemy vessels near the Norwegian coast. Ten ships were left burning, at a cost of three Beaus and three Mustangs. Pictured here is one of the escort vessels under heavy cannon and rocket assault./*British Official photo*

My association with Beaufighters began in September 1941 via the rather curious course of No.56 Squadron (Gauntlets); 802 Squadron (Nimrods) on *HMS Glorious* with the Mediterranean Fleet, and later Sea Gladiators; a unit of three Swordfish on floats (which I converted from an AACU to an operational unit at the beginning of the war); then a spell as operations officer at Group HQ, Gibraltar, to a twin-engine conversion course at Catfoss in September 1941. After conversion on Blenheims, and about 10 hours on Beaufighters, I was appointed CO of No 235 Squadron at Dyce in October '41. 235 was then equipped with Blenheims but had two Beaus on which the aircrews were slowly gaining a little flying time. As the squadron was still operational and maintaining regular reconnaissance patrols along the Norwegian coast, the rate of experience on Beaus was very slow. After a few weeks I had a phone call from the AOC, 18 Group. 'Did I know Sumburgh (Shetlands)?' –*Yes* – (*I'd been there about three times*) – 'Was it possible to operate Beaufighters at night from Sumburgh?' – '*Yes*' – 'Would *I* operate Beaufighters from Sumburgh at night, bearing in mind there was a 600 ft hill at one end of the runway, a 900 ft hill at the other, and the cross-runway was only 700 yards?' – '*Yes*' – 'OK, Tomorrow at first light fly all your Blenheims to Sumburgh, hand then over to 000 Squadron and take over their Beaufighters, and get them to Dyce and have your squadron operational as quickly as possible.'

Our flight from Sumburgh to Dyce, the immediate check on the aircraft, our signal saying it would take six weeks to get the aircraft operational – (the AM experts who were on the doorstep next morning disagreed – they said it would take *eight* weeks) – the frantic flying programme, the night I had done three circuits and landings (without lights) before Flying Control could be woken up, put on the lights and gave me permission to take off – all are part of a book in themselves! I had been hoping that we could slide into an operational role gently by way of Norwegian coast recces, Home Fleet escorts etc, but it did not work out that way. Another call from the AOC in late December, and on Christmas Eve we flew to Sumburgh for our first op. This was long range fighter cover for the Army and Navy in the first combined operation of its type – the Vaagso raid. Christmas Eve was very sober as we were due to operate next day. A 24-hours postponement brought another sober Christmas Day, made worse by the fact that the turkey we had had the forethought to bring with us had been stolen. On Boxing Day the job was 'on', and the narrative reads:

1st Sortie – 4 aircraft
1. Wg Cdr Garlick/Fg Off Payne
2. Flt Lt Wigmore/F/Sgt Crow
3. Sqn Ldr McConnell/Sgt Burnside
4. Plt Off Hughes/Sgt Myhill

Set course in formation 0859 – arrived Vaagso 1015 (just light) and took over patrol – 1030 sighted one Ju 88 which

made off – 1050 chased away a second Ju 88 – 1055 chased off one Me 109 – relief due 1145 but not sighted – 1203 vectored onto two low flying aircraft which turned out to be Me 109s – a hot 10 minutes for all concerned – Bill Hughes seen to dive in but not believed shot down – relieved 1210 – Wigmore chased by two more Me 109s on return journey – landed 1330.

2nd Sortie: 3 aircraft
1. Sqn Ldr Cook/F/Sgt Ludlow
2. Plt Off Chandler/Sgt Whitfield
3. Plt Off Austen/Sgt Hornsby

Set course 1200 – arrived Vaagso 1345 – patrolled until 1445 without incident (dusk) – landed 1600.

We had at least justified our claim that one could operate Beaufighters at night from Sumburgh, and kept enemy aircraft away from the naval and military forces, despite our inexperience on the type. I was most experienced with some 23 hours total flying time on Beaus – the least experienced had only eight and a half hours ...! For the next few months we continued to operate from Dyce – or rather, not to operate. For four weeks we spent all day clearing the runways of snow. A 'Dyce Operational' signal would go off each evening – and down would come the snow again. Finally the runways were bordered by six feet high banks of solid snow and ice before the weather let up. On March 20th, 1942 we moved to Sumburgh (in fact, one flight had been standing by for three weeks but there was never an occasion when both aerodromes were 'open') Because we were late in arriving,

we piled all our kit into the squadron offices – a wooden hut parallel to but set back about 50 feet from the runway. I was in bed in my half-Nissen hut quarters when the Tannoy (I had a speaker in my room) announced, 'Everyone is to get at least 400 yards from 235 Squadron offices. The torpedo is due to explode in seven minutes.' A quick telephone call confirmed that my hut was at least 400 yds from my office – wait for the bang – then out to inspect the hole surrounded by broken wood which had been my squadron offices. It was the result of a Beaufort returning from a routine torpedo patrol swinging on landing, hitting the hut and catching fire. No one was hurt but my squadron engineering officer did declare afterwards that the cubic capacity of the hut was insufficient to hold all the gear claimed as destroyed ...

There followed a period of routine recces of the Norwegian coast and the Faroes, Home Fleet escorts, punctuated by sudden detachments of two or three aircraft to Dyce or Wick to act as escorts to Beauforts in their torpedo attacks. During this period the *Tirpitz* was in Trondheim Fiord, the *Prinz Eugen* was expected to try to slip up the Norwegian coast to join her – and eventually did break free. So activity along the Norwegian coast was kept under close surveillance by PRU and Coastal Command recces, with fairly frequent escorted strikes by Beauforts. It was rarely that the whole squadron was in one place and there was a steady drain of aircraft that failed to return. This perhaps was one of the most unpleasant aspects – one rarely knew *why*. To quote an instance, a Beau on a routine Faroes patrol did not come back. True, the weather was bad – but it usually was. It was not until three months later that a boat fishing off Foula brought up an engine in its net, which was identified as from this aircraft. If you look at a chart of this area and calculate the chances of running slap into the vertical face of Foula in nil visibility, you will understand that the enemy was not our biggest problem.

One standby job we had – if Trondheim Fiord was cloud-covered so that the PRU could not take photos, we had to send a Beau at sea level, find the fiord entrance, go right up it and do a visual recce; not a prospect to look forward to. We only got called on to do it once. The weather was so foul I could not ask anyone else to do a job I wouldn't do myself, so muggins went. By sitting right on the wave tops (in fact, Bill Payne – my observer – complained his feet were getting wet), I could just keep the sea in view immediately in front of the nose. After over two hours flying and by dead reckoning within five miles of the coast, and visibility of not more than 200 yards, I gave up. When we got back the Met Officer said we had been through seven 'fronts'. Another visual recce was in cloudless conditions. *Prinz Eugen* had been reported in a fiord and PRU had no aircraft available. I went out at sea level, going below a Ju 88 obviously on standing patrol about 10 miles out to sea, climbed up the side of a mountain, popped over the top straight into flak from a largish ship and several escorts. Six Me 109s patrolling overhead turned towards me. As I reported when we got back, I couldn't identify the ship but it wasn't the *Prinz Eugen*, and this information seemed better than none. A lot has been made of the 'glamour' operations which hit the headlines, but in my view the toughest part was the routine slog, often in vile conditions, with a negative report at the end. One had to appreciate that if the job had been done properly, a negative report was often of greater value than a positive one.

In May 1942, twelve crews from 235 Squadron were ordered to proceed by boat and train to Lyneham to collect new aircraft and ferry them to the Middle East on posting. My instructions were to stay with one flight commander to 're-form' the squadron. The other flight commander was to accompany the party. They left in due course (their number having been increased to 14 in the

meantime) for their two-days journey. During the afternoon of the day they should have arrived at Lyneham, I received a call from the 18 Group controller asking where they were. I could only answer, presumably somewhere between Sumburgh and Lyneham. As the day wore on the calls kept coming in. The AOC, 18 Group wants to know . . . The C-in-C Coastal Command wants to know . . . the CAS wants to know . . . and finally, at 2am, Mr Churchill wants to know . . .! It was apparent that this was not a mere 'posting', and having spent time as a staff officer in the Ops Room at Gibraltar, it was clear to me why they were being 'posted' – cover for a Malta convoy. So I was not surprised when, within an hour of Mr Churchill's enquiry, I was told to take off at first light for Lyneham and take charge of the party. I got no further than Dyce before becoming weatherbound. Instead I was put on the afternoon train from Aberdeen, with Sqn Ldr Cook (the other flight commander, now going too), and arrived at Lyneham 24 hours later – to find that all the crews *had* reported and had been sent on 48 hours leave!

Our 'new' aircraft were the first produced by one of the 'shadow factories'. They were terrible. What should have been butt joints in the fuselage and wing plating over-lapped, inspection covers did not fit, screws were proud. Net result – top speed 30 knots *less* than our 'old' Beaus, and obviously an adverse effect on endurance, which would be of vital importance to us in our long two hops. (One aircraft had a complete Auxiliary Fire Service uniform stuffed in the wing behind the flaps! I've often wondered what happened to the fireman . . .) Guns had to be aligned, compasses swung, air tests carried out etc. I knew the urgency but as far as the station (Lyneham) was concerned we were just more transit crews. At any other station we could have manhandled the aircraft, but not at Lyneham. They were parked in sunken hangars, with a long ramp up to ground level, and only a tractor could get them out – and tractors were in short supply. I fumed – and finally a way to get things speeded up; by going straight over a lot of heads. The 'programme' then went:

June 3rd, 1942 – 16 aircraft left UK for Gibraltar – all arrived OK in about 4 hours 30 mins.
June 10th – Flew to Malta – took 5 hrs 50 mins (over normal safe endurance) – one aircraft missing.
June 14th – Four aircraft (pilots, Sqn Ldr

'LOCAL LABOUR' – Beau servicing on Malta, 1944; a sight seldom seen!/*M Kerr*

Above: **ON THE DRINK.**
Dorner 24 flying boat
'grounded' and under
continuing attack by
Beaufighters during a strike
against an enemy convoy north
of Crete./*Imperial War Museum*

Cook, Fg Off Eyre, Plt Off Downey, F/Sgt Crandell) protected the eastbound convoy for one and a half hours until dusk – Cook shot down one Ju 88. (By chance almost, I had gone to the briefing of the Spitfire pilots on this day. To my horror, I heard the briefing officer say, 'No problems about identifying aircraft. If it's twin-engined, it's *hostile*.' I was forced to point out the error of his ways . . .)

June 15th – Six aircraft (self, Fg Off Wood, Plt Off Cohen, F/Sgt Farquahar, Sgt Hall and Sgt Armitage) made R/V over convoy at dawn – almost immediately I sighted a force of two Italian cruisers and six destroyers steaming to intercept from the north – convoy alerted and sighting report sent to base – Italian force took up parallel course and lobbed in shells from long range – no air activity – Spitfires took over air cover – we made erratic sorties of two aircraft protecting torpedo aircraft – during these Sqn Ldr Wigmore destroyed an RO43 and damaged a Ju 88 – two further Ju 88s damaged by Cohen and Farquahar.

For the next six weeks we operated mainly as fighter cover for the Beauforts of 217 Squadron, led by Wg Cdr Davies, these operations being mainly on the Italian and Greek coasts, with occasional sorties off Tunisia, or on ships and landing craft between Sicily and the North African coast. If no strike was planned we were on immediate standby from first light until dusk. During this period our 'bag' increased by two Ju 88s and one SM79. Our co-operation with 217 Sqn developed beyond mere fighter cover. Whilst the Beauforts went in at sea level, we had a sub-flight at about 2,000 ft ready

to give close support and to make cannon and machine gun attacks on the ships; and another semi-flight at 4-8,000 ft (depending on the height from which we could keep the camouflaged Beauforts in sight – not an easy task). This flight, whilst providing top cover, went in on a straight and level course to simulate a bombing run – and on occasion we tossed out empty bottles which made a lovely whistling, screaming noise as they went down.

Life on Malta at this time was not particularly pleasant. Transport was almost non-existent (we were eating the gharry horses . . .) and, apart from the Army's purely operational work which included towing unexploded bombs off the airstrip and dumping them in a quarry, the only two cars I saw were those of the GOC and the AOC. The latter was AVM Sir Hugh Pugh Lloyd. Davies and I saw him quite often as our squadrons were a major part of his strike force, which he used effectively to deny the sea routes from Europe to North Africa to all shipping destined to supply Rommel at a vital stage in the war. Food was sparse – horse meat, goat, pork (not to be recommended in hot weather) and perhaps an egg for breakfast (a sure sign you were on an 'op' that day). No hot water – shaving was painful . . . Our quarters were in a single storey block without doors, windows or lights. Two to three beds in each room with a mosquito net – no other furniture. At night flying boots by the side of the bed, ready for feet to plunge straight into at the first crack of the 40mm Bofors outside the 'window'. Run down the corridor – dive into the

Above: **TWO'S COMPANY. A pair of 252 Squadron's early Beaus, 1941 when the unit pioneered the type in Coastal Command.**

shelter. That usually beat the first bomb, and happened two or three times a night. During the day two or three high level bombing raids by the Italians, plus Stuka attacks from time to time. The regular nightly raids, plus intruder operations, meant that returning to Malta after dark had a special flavour. No aircraft lights unless the controller gave permission, and quite often a case of 'lay-off' until called to come in – aerodrome lights restricted to 'fairy lights' along the runway which were only visible on actual approach – over the boundary and on came the floodlight – touch down, and out went the flood and all other lights. Then the only light to look for was a lighted cigarette being swung in circles by the airman waiting to guide you into the dispersal area. During the six weeks I was there we had no aircraft damaged by accident or by enemy action – ample tributes to the ground crews and the exceptional dispersal and blast wall protection. Four-gallon petrol cans filled with sand made excellent blast walls.

In July 1942, Sqn Ldr Cook, Flt Lt Payne and I returned by air to the UK, leaving the rest of the squadron to carry on the good work – which they certainly did. The return flight by Hudson, in shorts and shirt huddling into the mail bags to try to keep warm, was highly miserable. After leave I was posted as Chief Instructor to No 2 (C) OTU, a Beaufighter training unit. As my office was situated well out on the aerodrome, between the intersection of the runways, this was almost as good as another operational tour! On many occasions I hit the floor as Beaufighters 'swung' either

side of the office. Then in September 1943 I was posted as Controller at 16 Group HQ, Chatham, and for the year I was there the Beau Wing operating from North Coates carried out many brilliant attacks on shipping along the Dutch coast by Dan Helder.

Regarding the Beaufighter as an aircraft, those I flew were Mk 1 equipped with Hercules engines. This was the low level version built for Coastal Command, initially for long range recce, then long range fighter cover for Beaufort torpedo attacks, Fleet operations and combined Services ops. Its speed at sea level was sufficient to equal, if not outpace, the current Me 109; though with increasing height the 109 gained an advantage. Armament was six .303 machine guns and four 20mm cannons, all fixed and firing forward. Armoured glass windscreen, armour plate in front of the pilot and behind him. The poor Observer sat behind the rear armour plate, protected from frontal attack but with no rearward protection. With its short nose and the pilot high in front it provided a magnificent forward view for low level work. The engines were set forward so that their leading edge was in front of the cockpit. This, coupled with their weight and power, gave both advantages and disadvantages. The main disadvantage was a tendency to swing on take-off, which if not corrected immediately could become uncontrollable; and this resulted in many early Beaus wiping off their undercarriages or embedding themselves in other aircraft or in buildings. It also resulted in another trap for the unwary. If forced to abandon a landing and go round again, too sudden opening of the throttles flipped the aircraft upside down – few crews survived meeting the ground in this position.

Yet given these two traps for the unwary, the Beau was an extremely safe aircraft and one in which crew survival in a crash could almost be guaranteed *provided* the pilot cut both engines and went straight ahead, *regardless* of obstacles. The forward-placed engines battered obstructions out of the way, whilst the crew were encased in an armoured box, with the four cannons acting as skids. I have seen a Beau go through a copse of trees (scything them down), *through* the earthworks surrounding an ammunition hut, *through* the brick-built hut, and finish up literally as just an armoured box, with the pilot sustaining only a broken leg and his observer uninjured.

The Gallant 600

F W de VROOME BEM

BLACK KNIGHTS. Trio of 600 Squadron's Mk IF nightfighters on May 23rd, 1941, when the unit was based at Colerne, Wilts. The original photo shows evidence of the wartime censor's heavy hand, with nose and wing radar antennae 'brushed' out. */Imperial War Museum*

Amongst the earliest units to re-equip with Beaufighters was No 600 Squadron, AAF, who first received replacements for their out-dated Blenheim 'nightfighters' in September 1940. For the following two years 600's crews established a fighting record second to none, serving first in the UK and then moving at the end of 1942 to the Middle East, serving initially in Algiers. On June 24th, 1943, the unit's 20 Beaufighters were flown to the George Cross island – Malta – in advance preparation for the eventual Allied invasion of Sicily and the subsequent campaign in Italy. Dev de Vroome, the author of the following intimate account of 'the gallant 600's' men and deeds, was then serving as a SNCO with the squadron; and his esoteric descriptions of the many characters, both air and ground crews, reflect not only the atmosphere of the period but the typical contemporary humour.

Sicily

No campaign so decisive and so demanding in effort can be fairly reported in one article, without names and incidents getting more detailed mention. From the moment the squadron landed on the 'Hard' in Valetta, characters emerged in incidents in the air, on the ground, or down the 'Gut'. Within minutes of driving off an LST in a clapped-out Bedford bowser, one such made the elementary error of taking his eye off his kit, and within seconds his tunic was swiped. It would seem that that mythical character, 'Speedy Sicony', known to everyone one has served in Malta, had also emerged and was part of the committee of welcome. Whatever the welcome, we had arrived, and having been chosen by the Western Desert Air

Command for this task, time was precious and the opening rounds of the battle not far away. The operational flights moved into Luqa and set up HQ in a hut at the end of one of the two runways; while our maintenance echelon established themselves on the alternative aerodrome, Takali. Those echelon blokes, always in the background, deserve a special mention. Without the spur and satisfaction enjoyed by the flight erks when the tally of victories began to rise, and without the added pride of adorning their own 'bag of nails' with another swastika, they worked like Trojans. The squadron flew 1,000 operational hours in a month, plus a fair whack of day flying on escort or air-sea rescue searches, and with inspections of the aircraft occurring every 30 hours they were numerous. Warrant Officer Ben Opie, who met an untimely end in Naples a few months later, was in charge; assisted by Sergeants Maclean and Ginger Wheeley. The quality in performance was due in no small measure to a strong nucleus of Auxiliaries and pre-war VR's, and an unashamed name-dropping of some of the characters involved will support this modest praise in the memories of those who recall them. It was reputed that the only heat-treatment ever used in the workshop was to expose metals to the blistering wit of Wilf Hall, while in friendly altercation with Charlie De Lavigne and Joe Farley. Be that as it may, such redoubtable characters as Bob Hills, Bill Cooksey, 'Peter' Potter, 'Chippy' Chapman, George Nunn, Micky Noakes and Jack Wayne toiled right mightily through the heat and the gut-retching sickness that beset them, to produce the kites on time or before.

The flights were amalgamated for servicing and operations as far as aircraft were concerned, as practically everything not on inspection was needed each night. But the personnel were divided into A and B Flights for night ops, working alternate nights. These too had no slouches among them, and with such bods as Harry Dennis, Stan Cowell, George Hayhoe, Teddy Renton, Laurie Williams and Phil Spencer – to name just a few – Sgt Bert Chantrey and I had little to worry about in A Flight; whilst Sgts Fred Mayne and 'Barty' Bartholomew could hardly moan with Arthur Butterworth, Dai Williams, Bill Stapleton, Nobby Cockerton, 'Moggy' Cooke, Lofty Hutchinson and Ted Pellet as a fair sample in B Flight.

The day started early before the heat came on, and the squadron marched up from its camp among the ruins of Luqa village, because of the petrol shortage. The last lap up to the runway was uphill, and each morning the weary night crews would see the column march over the brow to the tune of 'There was a young lady from Hamm', sung by Frank Yates and 'Rube' Spink at the rear. Automatically there was an 'Eyes Left' to the nearest Beaufighter to see if the protecting fabric had been blasted off the gun ports, and we had been in business during the night. At the head of the column always was the discip man, Warrant Officer Fred Topping, whose broad red face has been described as almost everything down to a well-smacked backside. Once in sighting range, his eyebrows would shoot up in anxious question, and the crew to be relieved would signify the night's bag with an appropriate number of fingers. Some may have lingered on two fingers a little overlong, but as the import of the night's success was realised so 'Topper's' face would develop a ruddy beam from ear to ear, like a rising sun, and the step would pick up, as if the Central Band had struck up the RAF March Past. There was pride in everyone, pride in achievements, pride in the comradeship that charged each one, consciously or otherwise, with a determination that *his* day or night shift would be worthy of the one just done.

The day's first task was to scour the runway for scrap metal put up during the night by the Navy, Royal Artillery and the Malta Artillery. From previous experience, this trigger-happy trio would put up shot and shell with praiseworthy enthusiasm and gusto at the slightest provocation, not only to the discouragement of enemy raiders but also to anyone on our side sufficiently ill – advised to forget the colours of the day. After this morning constitutional the troops would get down to the major task of preparing the aircraft for the next round. Time was the all-important factor as the increasing heat made work inside the kites more difficult by the hour, until it became virtually impossible. This was particularly so for Cpl Doug Fell's instrument 'bashers', and the radio and radar bods of Sgt Colin Lamb and WO Pete Brown. By early afternoon we were geared up for action, and went into siesta until the night crews went on to limber up for the fight with night-flying tests (NFT's). Those not on duty would hie themselves to Valetta to join the social whirl of the 'Gut'. In common with everything else, there was a shortage of money on Malta, and the currency was made up with overprinted one-shilling notes, squares of lino representing pennies, postage stamps, and if these proved inadequate, cards printed, 'IOU 1/6d, Joe's Bar'. After a night of living it up on a rather odd brew of cola, labelled 'Port and Lemon' or 'Near Beer', and consorting with the local wenchery (whose conversation seemed limited to such profound statements as 'Up your pipe, Jack' and '.... my old gumboots'...), one could finish up with a fair start for the bathroom floor back in 'Blighty', and a nap hand of cards worth every cent of ten bob – if it were possible to remember where the hell they came from in the first place. Nevertheless, they made us right welcome – especially the watch repairers in Kingsway who, inundated with watches to be cleaned of the sands of Africa, discreetly closed down for two days prior to the Sicily D-Day (and, no doubt, flogged the spoils to our successors.)

Back at Luqa, the NFT's done, the decks were cleared for action, and with the dusk patrols began. Scarcely a night went by without the CO, Wg Cdr C.P. 'Paddy' Green and his operator, Fg Off Reg Gillies, being in the lead. If not in the air, the CO would direct operations from his ops caravan, converted from a kitchen trailer, complete with VHF aerodrome control etc and manned, seemingly at all times, by LAC 'Clubfoot' Coggins. Completely unflappable, immune to wrath, sarcasm or epithet, LAC Coggins performed a perfect 'Brad' to the CO's 'Harry Lime'. The battle was really joined and fought over Sicily, as Allied forces landed by sea and air on July 9th, 1943. The enemy concentrated his attacks during the night hours, and the squadron's victories in this campaign can

only be truly appreciated by those who have experienced the fruitless hours of toil in other times to achieve one or two successes during many months of night ops. Four destroyed in one sortie by Wg Cdr Green and Reg Gillies; three destroyed in 31 minutes by Sqn Ldr Desmond Hughes and Fg Off Dixon; three more in one sortie by Fg Off Johnny Turnbull and Flt Sgt Fowler – these were scores that any day fighter squadron could well be proud to record. But equal credit must be given to those other crews who did their respective stints with the same determination and whose results in determent of the enemy, if not recorded on the scoreboard, are established by the fact that the night air was cleared, and the landing and campaign in Sicily were

completely effective. Names like Hilken, Joe Hanus, 'Ace' Downing, Lyons, MacAnulty, Tait, Parkinson and Paton must act as proxy for those others who equally played their full part.

While this battle was being fought preparations for our impending move to Sicily were going on, as we had a 24-hour notice to cross over, as soon as a suitable strip was available. Finally on July 21st our airborne party landed at Cassibile, Sicily, where life became a little easier. This strip of volcanic dust was our own, self-contained and controlled, cut through the local vineyards and almond trees. We bedded both aircraft and ourselves in clearings among them and lived virtually cheek by jowl with our instruments of war. We were within easy reach of the sea, and most off-duty hours were spent in the 'drink', in the nude. This was no golden beach of a Mediterranean cruise brochure, but a rocky shore still strewn with the smashed wrecks of gliders of the airborne attack. Many of these had been cast off, in an offshore wind, by their American tug pilots, and had barely made it – several never did. Our prizes of war, captured from the Italians, enabled the strip to be fully equipped with landing T, revolving lighthouse, remote control flare path, and flood and funnel lights. Add to these a fire tender and ambulance, and we became a completely self-contained ops unit, able to take over any strip of dirt and operate immediately – our later role in the subsequent advance through Italy.

Enemy attacks continued steadily and our score mounted in consequence. The peak came on the night of a savage raid on Lentini, home of 244 Wing, DAF. Almost surrounded by dry grass and corn, it was vulnerable to fire, and most of it was set off by incendiaries. Ringed literally with fire, those Spitfire squadrons were trapped like rabbits in a harvest, but much of the final weight of the attack was fought off by the counterblast of our aircrews, who destroyed five and damaged another enough to dampen the enthusiasm of its crew. The toll on the resources of the Germans, already in retreat, in Ju 88s and He 111s must have been discouraging, and they changed their tactics by putting up single Ju 87s, usually with one within spitting distance of our strip, in the hope of clobbering us when the landing lights had inevitably to be used. With a low stalling speed, and high manoeuvrability, these were hard to nail, but it could be done, as demonstrated by Sqn Ldr Hughes and Fg Off Dixon, who put one down at Syracuse.

They also attracted much noisy attention from two AA barrages whose usual cone of fire seemed to be centred over our very exposed petrol dump. Nobody was very keen on this, especially the CO. Having acidly asked Frankie Yates if he was losing his nerve, when he found Frankie building a shelter out of rock in which to sleep, he forthwith instructed Warrant Officer Topping to have one built for him, for his limited sleeping hours. To recruit labour for this task, four unfortunate erks were nailed for 'extra duty' – for not having had a haircut! This, in the middle of nowhere, would seem a bit much, but since the only other source of amusement was to promote battles between rival nests of red and black ants, or single combat between a pair of beetles, it was received without resentment. Incidentally, the squadron champion beetle was one 'Hughes Hacker' who was retired undefeated when reduced to three legs by the combined efforts of the 'Blackwall Battler' and 'Blackwall Bruiser', owned and trained by Laurie Dixon and Reg Gillies respectively.

On the other side of the penny was an incident which typified the CO and the squadron he commanded. His Beau, 'F-Freddy', had developed hydraulic trouble, and with Laurie Williams, I'd worked into the night exchanging the master control valve. We were well satisfied but as the CO was off for the night, we'd wrapped it up for an air test in daylight. During the night HMS *Warspite* had been hit off Stromboli, and the squadron had been ordered to provide cover until dawn, while she made it back to port. The CO nominated himself for the job and, while lesser men would have shunned the un-tested 'F' pending daylight, he took it straight off and maintained the patrol until day came, without question or fuss. By the latter part of August the Sicilian campaign was wrapped up and preparations were made for the move to join the invasion of Italy, at Salerno. Our final task in Sicily was to train up the 415th Squadron, USAF, on Beaufighters, to take our place, but this exercise was mainly abortive. We rarely succeeded in getting them off the deck after dark, and their ground crews found the Beau far too complex. However, their tools and equipment were extremely good, and following a local lease-lend arrangement these stood us in good stead for the remainder of the war.

Southern Italy

With the completion of the campaign in Sicily, and the squadron score of 42 enemy aircraft destroyed and 10 pro-

Top left: **A-APPLE, a nine-victory veteran Beau of 600 Squadron, displaying a neat row of swastikas to mark its claims.**/*Imperial War Museum*

Centre left: **GONG CEREMONY. One of 600 Squadron's most successful crews, Plt Off A B Downing, DFM (rt) and Flt Sgt Johnny T Lyons, receiving an American Air Medal each from Major-General J House, commander of 12th Air Force Support Command, USAF. Tragically, Lyons was killed in action on February 1st, 1944.**/*Norman L R Franks*

Below: **With a lack of proper trestles, a ground crew utilizes a Coles Crane to hoist Beau JL899, 'Z' into flying position during major servicing on Malta. On the wing an armourer is harmonising the wing machine guns onto their marks on a harmonisation board (out of view).**/*Imperial War Museum*

bables in five weeks, the squadron was geared up to join 'Operation Avalanche' – the invasion of the Italian mainland at Salerno. The Eighth Army crossed the Straits of Messina and drove across to the Adriatic coast, taking Brindisi and swinging up to Bari. We went in with the British and American 5th Army, who had as a main target the capture of Naples, the primary objective being the established Italian airfield at Monte Corvino, scheduled for occupation on 'D-plus-2' – the day 600 Squadron advance party landed on Red Beach. The party, commanded by Flt Lt Hilken, consisted of 52 men armed for action, and 10 vehicles loaded to the roof with spares. Our prime object was to muster petrol and ammunition on the beach, and open up a dispersal area for our Beaufighters on 'D-plus-4'. This, however, was not quite on as the fighting went on for a week - the interim period being decidedly rugged. The leader of the opposition, Field Marshal Kesselring, was no slouch at the game and laid on quite a reception party, the crescent of hills being stiff with '88's' and the deadly accurate 'Minnies' that could pop a mortar bomb into your mess tin without touching the sides. In the course of this fighting, the aerodrome changed hands three times, but after heavy and costly battles, the field was finally taken on 'D-plus-8' and we were in business again. During this time the operational element of the squadron continued to give cover over both landings, and during the night of 'D-Day' found customers. Free-lancing over Salerno, three Ju 88s were shot down, the first by Flt Lt Johnny Turnbull and Fowler, and the other two by 'Ace' Downing and Johnny Lyons. The third Ea brought the overall total to date scored by the squadron to a round 100 destroyed. During those operations the Nav/Rad operators experienced some difficulty with their sets, and it was established that this was due to the first positive dropping of 'Window' by enemy aircraft. (This consisted of shreds of metal foil thrown out like confetti, which gave distorted blips on a radar set). At that time an AI 'Transponder' beacon was set up on the beach-head, and by the time the main squadron party arrived on September 26th, 1943, 12 Ju 88s, three He 111s and a Do 217 were shot down – two by Turnbull, three by Downing, four by Newhouse, three by Paton, and one each by Bates, Harrap, Young and Joe Hanus, the Czech. In this they were, of course, well assisted by their 'oppos' (Rad/Nav operators), and space must be given to

name them, as each victory was very much a team affair – Fowler, McAnulty, Tate, Lyons, Palfrey, Redmond, Finlay and Armstrong. We lost only one aircraft, of which the crew were saved.

Following the fighting the airfield was in a pretty ropey state, full of bomb and shell holes hastily filled in; and when the rains came it was often unserviceable. In spite of the problems of aircraft sinking up to their engine nacelles at times in the mud, patrols were maintained over Naples from Monte Corvino, and over Brindisi from a detachment at Bari, 'led' by Warrant Officer 'Twinkle' Nelson (whom Heaven preserve, if the alcohol hasn't already done so . . .) The weather deteriorated and eventually rain and mud rendered the airfield almost unserviceable. As a stop-gap, Bert Chantrey and I took a detachment to Gando, continuing the operations by night, though for a month there was no opposition until they pushed their luck on October 24th and Watson and Paton 'fixed' a Ju 88 each. During this lull WO Fred Topping and Sgt 'Rube' Spink organised a first class camp at Monte Corvino, and everyone was in the lap of luxury. Tent lines were built in the orange groves – named after city of London streets, the name-plates being painted in authentic style and detail by Cpl George Redding. Bed boards were found for everyone, 'banjo fires' and other ominous heating appliances were built using local initiative, and the electricians managed to install a lighting system in every tent. With the arrival of NAAFI stores, the squadron found itself enjoying its second Christmas overseas in comparative luxury. About this time Italy capitulated and the bedraggled remnants of Mussolini's 'Three Million Shining Bayonets' started walking home. Many a good bargain was struck for the odd watch etc and found its way to Blighty, until we were informed from a very high level that the Italians were no longer a defeated enemy, but were now our Allies! (You could have fooled us, but not to be bitter and twisted – it takes all sorts to make a war . . .)

At this time too was founded the 'Hurricane Club'. This had no connection with any other enterprise of the same name, and let its exploits not besmirch the revered memory of the old thoroughbred. In the camp 'Lights Out' was at 2200 hours, so the sergeants' mess won itself a hurricane lamp. One member was 'Duty Aladdin' on the mess roster each week, and at 2159 hours stood ready. At 'Lights Out' the lamp was duly lit, all

initiated members chanting, 'Jesus bids us shine with a pure, pure light', accompanied on the piano (swiped from Batapaglia railway station sidings). By now many of our experienced and successful crews were running out of time, and in spite of 'operational extensions' organised by Paddy Green, eventually they had to go home. Their replacements were comparatively 'green', and a training flight was set up under the leadership of Sqn Ldr Angus Horne (who earned himself the distinction of being awarded both the DFC and AFC with the squadron.) This flight operated mainly from Foggia/Tortorella and brought new crews up to the demanding standard of the CO and the task in hand.

Since the Luftwaffe appeared to dislike either the rain or the treatment it had been getting, it appeared very shy; so the squadron took on an additional role of seeking it out at home in the New Year, 1944. In addition to the patrols flown from Gaudo, intruder operations were flown from Tortorella into the Rimini-Bologna sector in the north, and though no enemy aircraft were destroyed much havoc was created amongst the enemy's rail and road transport. The weather had not helped the 5th Army any more than it had us, so at the first real break another landing was mounted to shorten the lines to Rome – at Anzio. This livened things up more than somewhat and in the first few days of the landing, 11 enemy aircraft were shot down over the beach-head. Warrant Officer Harrup got two, Sqn Ldr Horne two, Flt Lt Hilken two, Paddy Green (the CO) got one, Flt Lt Turnbull had one, and the irrepressible 'Ace' Downing and his partner-in-crime Johnny Lyons got three in one sortie. Intensive use of 'Window' made interception extremely difficult, and since both sides were very free with their disposition of flak over the fighting area, these victories were particularly hard to come by. It was now decided to move the squadron forward to Marchianese, north of Naples, which is another story altogether because from there our role changed to the highly mobile unit we remained for the rest of the war. Therefore to conclude this earlier phase of the 'Gallant 600's' exploits, it must be said that both in the air and on the ground, the squadron had won the respect of its contemporaries, had earned the title in the UK press of the 'Gong Squadron' for its many awards, and a score of at least 101 enemy aircraft destroyed, for the loss of only two crews during its overseas service.

Combat Report

Combat Report 1

225 Squadron. Night 27/28 May 1943
Fg Off T. A. O'Sullivan (pilot); Sgt W. G. Hood (Rad/Nav)
Resta 30. Beaufighter VIF,V8510. Four cannon; six mgs Mk IV A.I.
Took off 20.45 from La Sebala 2: Landed there 22.50.

On dusk patrol for 'Mixture' at 10,000 ft. Over to 'Spongebag' who reported 5-10 bogeys to NE crossing SW to Bizerte. No height given. 'Spongebag' brought Beaufighter in behind, losing height to 8,000 ft. Contact obtained at 8,000 ft range to port and a little above. Closed very rapidly to 3,000 ft and identified Ju 88 by silhouette against light sky in west. Closed to 80-100 yards a little below and dead astern. Now 15-20 miles NE of Bizerte at approx 21.10 hrs an attempt was made to open fire but it was not until the firing button had been manipulated in various positions for 10-15 seconds that a one-second burst was given with all guns. The starboard engine of Ea immediately burst into flames. As Ju 88 broke away to port the rear gunner opened fire without damaging the Beaufighter. The visual was lost but contact held. Ea was taking evasive action but Beaufighter was brought into 1,500 ft and visual was obtained. A little flame and large amount of grey smoke could be seen coming from starboard engine. Ea was doing tight turns and had lost height to 6,000 ft. A full deflection one-second burst was given at 60 yards range. Ea port engine exploded and strikes were seen on fuselage. Ea went down vertically into the sea and disappeared. No one seen to bale out.

Rad Nav found he had another contact at 4,000 ft range, above and well to starboard. Closed to 2,000 ft and identified as Ju 88 by silhouette against the light western sky. At 100 yards range from dead astern and slightly below, a two-second burst was given from all guns. EA's starboard engine exploded and strikes were seen on fuselage. Ea dived vertically into sea. Two more explosions seen in the engine before the aircraft went down.

'Spongebag' had nothing more, so Beaufighter patrolled NW-SE, just off Bizerte. Several vectors were given in NE direction after a bandit returning from target area. Followed it for 80 miles until 'Spongebag' could give no further help. Returned to patrol line. Put onto bogey when about 40 miles from coast. After two minutes' chase, control said it was friendly.

Weather: Cloudless over Bizerte area. 10/10ths cloud 60 miles out to sea. Top, 10,000 ft.
Rounds fired:
Two cannons did not fire – dust in breech
One cannon fired 10 rds – oversized rd
One cannon fired 50 rds
MGs fired 60 rds each.
CLAIM: Two Ju 88s Destroyed.

Combat Report 2

255 Squadron. Night 11/12 May 1943
Pilot: Fg Off K. T. A. O'Sullivan; Rad/
Nav, Sgt W. G. Hood
Resta 30. Beaufighter VIF V8518.
Took off 22.25 hrs from Paddington;
landed there 00.50.

Patrolled under 'Brownie' and 'Donald'
east of Bizerte at 10,000 ft until 23.45 hrs.
Under 'Donald' put onto a bogey travelling west taking evasive action. Fleeting
contact well out to starboard at max
range, lost immediately. Hard turn to
starboard given by control onto 260
degrees. Contact obtained again well to
starboard. At 170 mph IAS closed in
rapidly to 3,000 ft, losing height to 7,500
ft. The evasive action of Ea was followed
accurately by Radio Nav. A visual was
obtained of exhausts at 3,000 ft. Closing
to 120 yards the Ea was identified as an
He 111 by silhouette and position of exhausts. At approximately 00.10 hrs when
near Bizerte fire was opened at 100-120
yards range with a one-second burst with
cannons only, strikes being seen on the
fuselage. For three seconds there was inaccurate return fire from the mid-under
position. This ceased when a one-second
deflection burst from the Beau hit the
port engine, which exploded, debris flying
past our aircraft. A third one-second
burst from the same range caused an explosion in the fuselage. The enemy aircraft went to starboard, giving off flames
and a great amount of smoke, finally
hitting the ground and exploding. No one
was seen to bale out. The Beaufighter
orbitted for a time and then returned to
base.
Weather: Fine, no cloud. Moonlight.
Visibility good, but difficult to dis-
tinguish land from sea.
Rounds fired:
   30 each from 3 cannons
   20 from one cannon (lack of tension on
BFM)
   MGs not used.
CLAIM: One He 111 Destroyed.

Right: 255 Squadron, B Flight air crews, Sicily, September 1943. Back row, L-R: Flt Sgts Robertson; Philipps; Hale; Pollard; Williams; Hewitt; WO Walker; Flt Sgt Hilliard; WO Streeter; Flt Sgt Izonsky. Front row: Fg Offs Humphreys; Watson; McGugan; Phillips; Sqn Ldr P H V Wells, DSO; Fg Offs D Carter; Nichols; Berry; Sparg. On grd; Fg Offs Porter and G Carter.

Below: Beaufighter Mk IIF, R2402, YD-G of 255 Squadron, seen at Coltishall in September 1941. It later served with 410 Squadron./*Bristol Aeroplane Company*

Italian Nights

TIM REYNOLDS

Above: **Two views of a Beau Mk VIF of the 1st Tactical Air Force, USAF. The 'thimble' nose radome housed the improved Mk VIII A.I. equipment.**/*Imperial War Museum*

When I finally came to fly Beaus I had already completed a tour on Blenheims in North Africa, and as a 'rest' was attached to the Communications Flight of 242 Group, MACAF, at Bizerta. This moved with the Group to Taranto and I became Personal Assistant (PA) to the AOC, Air Cmdre 'Bing' Cross (much later, C-in-C Bomber Command in the UK). I stuck this job for two-three months and finally managed to wangle a posting to a night fighter squadron (255) in the Group, at Grotaglie, near Taranto. I must have been lucky to have been accepted as a pilot because at that time I had never touched a Beaufighter VIF in my life, but perhaps the AOC had put in a good word for me as I was obviously desperate to get away from the PA's job! Luckily too the CO was sympathetic and, in view of my 'twin' training and time on Blenheims, decided to let me have a go. At this stage of my flying career, apart from Blenheims, I had flown some 30 or so different types, including Spits, Hurris, Venturas, Marylands, DC3s, Bostons and even a Fieseler *'Storch'* in my capacity as OC Comm Flight, and latterly as PA to the AOC. This I think enabled me to take on

the Beau with an open mind, plus a sincere attraction for night flying in general. Having had a couple of trips in daylight standing behind my flight commander, Pat Wells, he sent me off solo. Right from that moment I fell in love with the Beau and, having got used to the considerable extra power vis-a-vis the Blenheim, things seem to work out quite well on that trip, and I managed to get down in one piece. The major problem of night flying, and indeed night fighting, came next, and with a bit of luck and a lot of help from my radio navigator, Mike Wingham, I managed to learn about the secrets of airborne radar and night interceptions. Mike was probably one of the best R/O's on the squadron and soon after I joined 255 his pilot went tour-ex and I snapped him up. From there it seemed a short step to patrol duties over the Adriatic and eventually the squadron moved to Foggia, with detachments at Malta, Taranto, Naples and, later, Ancona.

All this time I was gradually getting to know my aircraft better and better. I had managed soon after becoming operational (through becoming friendly with the squadron engineer Officer, Roy Laver) to have a new aeroplane allotted to me, which I collected direct from the Maintenance Unit (MU) in Algeria, and which (of course) was lettered 'R-for-Reynolds' (KW154, YD-R). I succeeded in retaining this Beau throughout my stay with 255, and I don't think anyone else actually flew it during that time. With Roy Laver's help I managed to get it more or less on top line but not before he had had to have the port outer wing section changed to cure its habit of flying port wing low, and at the same time fitting a complete new tail unit to stop the thing yawing – all whilst I was trying to sort out the guns! What it is to have friends . . .

At this point I think I must make it clear that to succeed from a night fighting point of view, it was imperative to know your own aircraft like the back of your hand. In other words you had to recognise its shortcomings regarding speed, handling, behaviour under full power, its stability as a gun platform, and of course the characteristics of the guns themselves – not to mention oil and fuel consumptions, engine performance and general idiosyncracies. Above all you *had* to be absolutely on the same wavelength as your RO – this decided whether it was to be success or failure. If he was unable to make you aware of what was happening out there almost before it happened, or you were unable to translate

Above: **SPRINGBOKS. Crews of 16 Squadron SAAF, Balkan Air Force, seated on their PSP (Pierced Steel Planking) 'runway' in front of a Beau Mk X, loaded with 3-inch RP, prior to a sortie, 1945.**/*Imperial War Museum*

his commentary into instant action, all your knowledge of your aircraft and your flying skill was wasted. Needless to emphasise, Mike and I had an understanding which I think bordered on the telepathic and for that main reason we were moderately successful.

Coming now to 'R-Reynolds', which after all was the only Beau VIF I was intimate with – I *flew* several others, but I actually fought in 'R' – it was pretty reliable throughout the time in spite of the fairly hard life to which it was subjected. Apart from unsurfaced runways, primitive servicing facilities, dust, heat, and long hours in the air; it occasionally was asked to have a go when the odd unidentified target turned up. One such night we chased a Hun for nearly an hour at full throttle at low level, but he got away thanks to his nitrous oxide injection system (we thought it was a Junkers 88). Poor old 'R' did its best but the following day the port engine had to be changed because the plugs were welded into the cylinder heads and couldn't be shifted – all 36 of 'em... The next time this gentleman appeared we had a bit more warning and instead of a 'stern chase' we

were vectored onto a proper interception course and caught him at about 50 feet above the sea. It was a Ju 88 and was equipped with a radio altimeter which was accurate down to three metres. Our own aneroid altimeter was useless below 100 feet and we didn't get radio ones for at least three months after this event. The technique was to dive on him while he was low on the water and try to force him up by firing short bursts in the dive. One such burst got him in the fuselage tank... All this time our airborne radar – Mk VIII A.I. – had been working excellently, and I think our own personal 'best' was an air-to-air interception at night of $12\frac{1}{2}$ miles at about 8,000 feet This equipment was highly secret at that time and was streets ahead of anything the Germans had. The whole time we were operating on night interceptions I don't think it ever let us down at a critical moment, which is saying something for such a complicated piece of equipment. (Thinking back, I can't remember ever having to cut a patrol short due to engine problems either.)

Our next three kills were all Ju 87s (two in one night) which, as can be imagined,

were very different types of target. They could practically *hover* compared with a Beau, and if it had not been for the excellent forward visibility from a Beau pilot's seat we should have lost them time and time again. The Beau in this respect was magnificent, as I discovered to my cost when I eventually flew Mosquitos and had great difficulty in seeing through their rather odd-shaped and remote screen. Likewise, the Beau's slow-flying capabilities were quite reasonable enough, although the sight of us wallowing along behind a Ju 87 with full flap, undercart down, fully-fine pitch and *still* over-shooting the target had to be seen to be believed. It was not the world's most stable gun platform at this speed. The final kill is hardly worth recording except that it proves how deadly the Beau's armament was if the target was caught exactly in the 'cone' (of fire) – approximately 300 yards ahead. We caught a Ju 88 flying *straight and level* into the dawn one morning over the Adriatic, and it only needed 12 rounds per cannon and 24 rounds per machine gun to sort him out. Not very heroic . . .

One other night interception story illustrates probably what I found to be the only shortcoming where the Beau was concerned – lack of power above 20,000 feet. We had had a lot of trouble trying to

Top: **BALKAN BEAUS.** 16 Squadron SAAF duo, nearest NV139, 'Z', over Yugoslavian hill country en route to target, 1945./*Imperial War Museum*

Above: RD162 of an unidentified unit returning from a rocket sortie, Yugoslavia./*via S G Jones*

Right: **BLOCK BUSTERS.** SAAF Beaus of the Balkan Air Force attacking enemy-occupied barracks at Postumia, 23 miles east of Trieste, on March 23rd, 1945. They scored at least 84 direct hits with their rockets, leaving most barrack blocks devastated and/or burning./*British Official photo*

Top right: **Three views which tell a complete story.** On September 24th, 1944, eight Beaus from 272 Squadron attacked the Italian liner 'Rex', which was about to be used as a blockship in Trieste harbour. The giant liner sustained a total of 123 3-inch RP hits and sank. Photos show (i) the 'Rex' under attack; (ii) after attack; and (iii) the Beau crews of 272 Squadron responsible./*E G Myring, DFC*

Bottom right: **TUG TARGET.** An enemy tug, just after leaving the Greek port of Preveza on October 7th, 1944, receives the full blast of a Beau's cannons./*British Official photo*

down a night photo-recce Hun who kept
flying over Taranto at around 25,000 feet
photographing the harbour installations
and ships at regular intervals which,
although way above our normal
operational height, we thought we could
intercept given a bit of warning when,
say, he was crossing the Adriatic on his
way from his base in Albania. It fell to our
lot to be on patrol that particular night
and, as previously agreed, we climbed on
course to interception height. It must
have taken a full hour at full throttle and
maximum supercharger power (the
Hercules engines had two-speed blowers
with manual control) to get to 25,000 feet.
After wallowing around at that height
literally hanging on our props, we were
told by our ground station that they had
got a contact slightly below and about
eight miles away. We turned towards it
on their instructions with very great
difficulty as the Beau would hardly
answer the helm, and then saw the flash
'bombs' exploding (magnesium flares
suspended from parachutes) below us. At
that moment Mike got a contact on our
own radar at about four miles and told me
to turn towards it and to start going down
– much to my relief. The speed started to
build up and at this stage I remember
isolating the ground station VHF trans-
missions with a special switch which
stopped any interference with Mike's
commentary. (The ground controller told
me afterwards that he was petrified to see
us gradually going faster and faster at an
ever-increasing angle towards the sea,
and there was nothing he could do about
it.) Mike by now had a perfect contact
and we continued diving after it. I
remember checking the ASI and
altimeter on the way down and which
were approaching 300mph and 10,000 feet
respectively at that moment. The next instruction from Mike was, 'SLOW DOWN
– WE'RE OVER-SHOOTING – SLOW!'
Whereupon I became very busy as nobody
likes overshooting a target in case you
suddenly find you are being chased instead. I did my best to get rid of all that
lovely speed which we'd built up by
throttling right back, going into fine pitch
(gingerly. . .), putting the undercart down
(both pairs of doors disappeared with a
bang, naturally), flaps as soon as the
speed was right, and finally a quick
glance at the altimeter – it was just
coming up very fast to ZERO FEET. I
looked up, saw the moonpath reflected on
the sea approaching very rapidly, and
heaved on the stick literally with both
feet braced on the ledge below the instrument panel. We skimmed the water

Above: **Float version of the 'Iron Annie' (Junkers 52) set ablaze on the water near Thermia, Greece, 1943 by a roving Beaufighter.**/*Imperial War Museum*

Right: **Magnificent view of a 16 Squadron SAAF Beau, 'K', releasing a full salvo of 3-inch RP against German barracks at Zuzemberk, Yugoslavia, early 1945.**/*SAAF Official*

without an inch to spare and rocketed back up to 3,000 feet with everything off and back. Although I blacked out momentarily, it says much for the dear old Beau's strength to withstand that dive and the pull-out without flinching. What a kite. . .

It took a long time to fathom out what had happened – all sorts of 'helpful' suggestions were made by all and sundry, like 'You must have chased one of his long-range tanks' – but finally Mike admitted (in his cups, one night on leave) that at the height we were flying that night he was not getting any 'ground returns' (radar echoes caused by the bottom of the cone transmitted by the scanner in the aircraft nose being reflected by the ground and giving a signal on the tube), but as soon as the nose of the Beau dipped he saw what he thought was a blip from the Hun aircraft. This was in fact the echo from the sea between four and five miles below us, which caught him unawares and which he then proceeded to chase thinking the target was trying to get away by diving down almost vertically ... 'nuff said; except that a Mossie was called in from a Malta squadron and shot the high-flyer down the next time it appeared.

Apart from covering the Anzio beachhead, being 'snowed on' by lava from Vesuvius when it erupted, and doing a wheels-up landing (due to a burst tyre on take-off), nothing much else happened until we were sent over the Danube on night intruder work. Once again the Beau

proved itself very adaptable and ideal for the job in hand, particularly the weight of armament and, of course, superb forward visibility. We lost very few aircraft and had a certain amount of success with 'R'. Mike's sense of direction was superb and his navigation equally good. It was not easy map-reading at night at very low level over a strange country, with dodgy maps and no radio aids. The only problem I found with night attacks was to know when to break off the attack to avoid bouncing off the deck – the temptation was to keep the nose down as long as possible to maintain effective saturation of the target with cannon, but at the same time to allow for a certain amount of 'mush' when the nose was pulled up – easily misjudged, particularly if the horizon was obscured or absent altogether. On top of this, the angle of dive always seemed much steeper than it probably was, but on the other hand when you consider that the Beau's guns were aimed to converge at a point approximately 250 – 300 yards dead ahead, it is not difficult to imagine how steep the dive had to be to bring them to bear on a stationary target.

When I left 255 Squadron I stayed in the Middle East for a while, teaching Americans to fly Beaufighters, ferrying the odd VIP around, and finally discovering that a tour-expired Beau – without armament or radar – could *not* maintain height on one engine (although it could, and was, barrel-rolled on two) which resulted in having to ditch it in Gibraltar

harbour where it promptly sank in something like 45 seconds; taking with it a chum who I'd known since boyhood and who came up with me to see what a Beau was like. I was out in a flash from the cockpit hatch, but he was stunned and didn't make it. The single engine non-sense was caused by the failure of the port feathering motor which I had been asked to test and the prop had stopped half-way between 'feathered' and 'unfeathered'. The maintenance crew had failed to do a simple modification to the feathering motor pressure pipe to stop it chafing against the bulkhead, and it burst where it was worn – simple as that. I returned to the UK shortly afterwards and on my first flight since the accident, I had *just* got the wheels up after taking off at Charter Hall (Berwickshire) when the port engine's oil pressure disappeared off the clock, there was a loud bang and then no power on the port side. I though that things were not looking too rosy at that moment but I went through the drill, like feathering the port prop, and – guess what? – the feathering pipe burst.

I thought, 'No chance of ditching in Scotland' but remembered that all the trouble started on the previous trip when I put the wheels down (I couldn't raise them again in time because of the lack of hydraulic power from only one engine); so, in spite of quite a bit of drag from the partially feathered prop, I left undercart and flaps well alone and managed to coax a little height, like 300 feet, out of the beast. I made a circuit and approach (into the dead engine, of course) which must have been all of 10 miles long, and ginger-ly lowered the wheels and flaps practical-ly over the boundary. I must have touched down just as the wheels locked but everything was OK.

What annoyed me more than anything, apart from the waste of a life on the previous trip, was the failure of the same pipe on the second trip for the very same reason – the mod had not been done. When I recovered from the shock I saw the engine being changed in the corner of the airfield, presumably to get it away before it could be inspected, and in high dudgeon (as they say) I paid the senior engineering officer a visit and told him what I thought was going on, and please, I wasn't trying to 'revenge' my chum's death, but could he do something drastic to stop any more 'nasties' – which to his credit he did. That was the end of my personal Beau saga, and from then on I started flying Mossies – that's another story...

69

Strike on Cos

E J LEDWIDGE

Ledwidge's war was in many ways the pattern for so many Beaufighter crews. Years of flying and operating in varying climates, against a wide variety of objectives – the epitome of the 'unsung' crews who provided the bulk of success in every facet of the air war. His first tour of operations was with 409 Squadron in the UK, piloting Defiants, then Beaufighters in the night interceptor role, under the inspiring command of the Canadian Wing Commander Paul Davoud. In eight months with the Canadians, Ledwidge flew many sorties but with no positive 'kill' to record – an experience shared with most of his squadron. Not that this tour was without incident, and on at least one local co-operation sortie he had the almost unique 'privilege' of flying with an LACW WAAF as his *official* radar operator! His second operational tour commenced in September 1942, with 46

(Uganda) Squadron, flying various marks of Beaus in the Middle East theatre. Like all desert Beau units, 46 Squadron's duties were many and varied – night interception, ground-strafing, anti-shipping et al. During a year's operations with 46, Ledwidge participated in every type of sortie undertaken by the squadron, culminating in a particularly dangerous strike against a German invasion force attacking the Allied-occupied island of Cos on October 3rd, 1943. On that date 46 Squadron suffered tragic losses, including their commander, Wing Commander G. A. Reid. One of the 'losses' was Ledwidge's Beaufighter. The following personal account of his experiences on that and subsequent days fails to mention that he was later awarded a DFC for this and the many other operations he had flown.

BOMBS GONE. Beau-bomber attacking two enemy F-boats south of Kalino, in the Dodecanese, on October 18th, 1943. By the later stages of the war many Beaus were modified to carry two 500lb HE bombs under the fuselage, and/or two further bombs under the wings./*Imperial War Museum*

'It was Sunday morning, my day off, when I was awakened by someone coming into my tent and telling me that I was required immediately, and to report to the briefing officer with my navigator. Evidently there was a big 'do' on and several of the squadron's Beaufighters had gone missing on a shipping strike earlier in the morning, including our CO's. On arrival at the briefing tent, the Intelligence officer told us that a German invasion fleet was sweeping south through the Aegean Sea, recapturing the islands and moving towards Cyprus. Apparently our CO, Wg Cdr Reid, had been shot down whilst taking part in an earlier strike by six Beaus off the island of Cos. I had recently lost my usual navigator, Flight Sergeant 'Chick' Bonner, after he'd been severely injured during a night attack on September 11th against the Maratza airfield in Rhodes. Our aircraft had been hit by the exploding bombs of another Beau as we inadvertently flew over them during our run-in on the airfield; so my new navigator, Flight Sergeant Rowlay, was about to take part in his first operational strike. According to the briefing officer the German force was composed of several large vessels as troopships, defended by a number of flak ships and various other ships, including destroyers and E-boats, plus a number of landing barges etc. At the time these were attempting a landing on the island of Cos, where there was a squadron of Spitfires on the small airfield, supported by a detachment of the Durham Light Infantry, as well as a large number of Italian troops

Top left and right: **Views of Flt Lt Ledwidge's personal Beau, T5273, of 46 Squadron, at Edcru, Egypt, December 1942. First view shows the Beau with its temporary nickname, 'BENGHAZI BUS' on Christmas Eve, 1942, prior to conveying a load of traditional Christmas fare. Second and third photos give close-ups of (a) the chalk soubriquet on that occasion, with Ledwidge standing in his cockpit; and (b) the more permanent title of the machine, 'ANNIE' (after his wife) tastefully inscribed on its rudder.**/*Flt Lt E J Ledwidge, DFC*

Bottom left: **Flight Sergeant (then) E J Ledwidge, 46 Squadron, in his 'office', Benghazi, 1942.**/*Flt Lt E J Ledwidge, DFC*

Above: **ANNIE WAS A LADY. T5273, 46 Squadron en route to Benghazi, December 1942, piloted by E J Ledwidge.**/*Flt Lt E J Ledwidge, DFC*

who were now 'on our side' since the capture of the island months before and the final capitulation of all Italian forces in the Middle East area.

Other Beaufighter squadrons were sharing in these proposed strikes, including 252 and 272 and a few crews from 89 Squadron. Following the briefing, four of our Beaus, led by Squadron Leader Bill Cuddie (a Canadian), myself in Beau JL903, 'N', as his No.2, and another pair flown by Sgts Holmes and Jackson (an Australian), took off and set course at low level across the sea towards Cos. Our briefing had disclosed that enemy forces were on the south side of the island, consisting of a small number of landing barges with a couple of flak ships, but that the main force was thought by then to have continued southwards. Our task was to attack the barges if they were still in the vicinity. In the Beaufighter I had a habit of using the main fuel tanks in the wings close to the fuselage as soon as we were airborne and during the outbound trip. I had a theory that there would be less risk of a serious explosion if we were hit in combat as most of the fuel would be in the outer tanks, well away from the fuselage. As things turned out my theory proved correct – at least as far as this trip was concerned.

Approaching the island from the south there appeared to be no activity and there were only a couple of beached barges left stranded and deserted on the shoreline, with no sign of life. Bill Cuddie then came over the R/T, 'Let's see what's on the other side', so we flew across the island and the deserted airfield south-west of the high ground. As we reached the sea on the north side of the island, away to our north-east, lying off the harbour, was the whole of the invasion fleet! Obviously the island had been recaptured and the enemy was busy either off-loading more troops or taking stores to or from the harbour. As soon as we saw them Bill Cuddie called, 'There they are – let's have a go at that lot.' Throttles up smartly to combat setting, friction nut screwed up tight, and we were closing in on the ships – spreading out slightly to present a more difficult target and thereby leaving room for the Beaus to weave as each of us selected individual targets. We carried two 250lb bombs (three seconds fused) on each Beau and as we closed in I remember thinking, 'Mustn't forget to fuse the bombs before we drop 'em. . .'

We were about a mile from the ships when they started to fire at us and the puffs of black smoke, with the associated churning up of the water beneath the ex-

SIESTA. Flight Sergeant E J Ledwidge 'resting' on the propeller of Beau X7716, 'R' of 46 Sqn, Benghazi, 1942. This particular Beau had earlier seen operational service with 89 Squadron./*Flt Lt E J Ledwidge, DFC*

ploding shells, gave me the usual impression that all the shrapnel exploded downwards and that if one flew above the shell bursts one would be safer – highly wishful thinking, of course. As we approached the flak was in layers and I subconsciously weaved up and down between the layers. Suddenly Bill Cuddie's Beau veered sharply to the right in front of me and as it did so exploded in a great orange and black cloud immediately ahead. As I pulled sharply upwards to avoid the explosion I clearly remember the sight of that great pall of black smoke with the light shining brightly on the sea just beneath. We were now on top of the outer extremity of the ships, above the destroyers and flak ships which were in a defensive ring around the motor vessels. Having zoomed up to avoid the exploding aircraft, I found myself almost over the ring of defending vessels at about 400 to 500 feet above a destroyer. I had to pull the Beau hard into a wing-over to bring my guns to bear on this ship. Through the gunsight I could see the churning of the water caused by my cannon shells as they ran up to and finally sprayed across the stern of the destroyer. As I began to pull hard to the right towards the motor vessels, there was a brilliant flash of an explosion and the whole rear part of the destroyer blew apart (I suppose I must have hit some depth charges). The force of the blast almost hurled the aircraft over onto its back in a roll to the right.

On pulling out I found myself heading directly towards the middle one of three

big ships and as my cannon shells sprayed the side of the ship I could see grey figures moving away each side of the shell strikes. I released my bombs and pulled up over the funnels of the motor vessel – and then noticed a smell of burning cellulose. We had obviously been hit but that was the last thing one thought – it must be the electrics, or the radio equipment, and anyway the aircraft was still flying all right . . . My nav called over the intercom that he too could smell something burning, and that an Arado floatplane was firing at us from just above. Throughout the attack it was obvious that we were receiving hits of some sort, and we could still hear thumps and bangs around the aircraft. All I could do at this time was to keep corkscrewing the Beau to make a more difficult target for the guns, and my navigator felt the same way for he repeated over and over 'Keep weaving, the shell bursts are still close.' During the final part of the attack as we approached the MVs in the centre of the melee, I noticed Sgt Holmes' aircraft on a parallel course to me and saw his bombs drop straight towards the MV to our left and now, as we were weaving away low over the sea, there he was, still on a parallel course, streaking across the water with one of his engines pouring black smoke. I remarked to my nav, 'I wonder how far he'll get with that engine trouble?' It was obvious he wouldn't make it back to base. The nav then informed me that fuel was pouring past him on the starboard side and I thought, 'Let's hope our outer tank hasn't been holed' because we needed all that fuel to get back to base. However, the nav confirmed that the fuel was coming from the inner tank. I looked out over the starboard wing and saw little damage apart from a buckled panel and a couple of small holes about midway along the wing. But the smell of burning had become much stronger and seemed to be coming from somewhere inside the fuselage. By this time we were clear of the flak and flying low towards the Turkish mainland, with Sgt Holmes about half a mile to our left, still streaming smoke. Dead ahead of us at about 10 miles I could see what appeared to be a mosque with a tall white tower.

My navigator then decided to come up through the fuselage to see if he could trace the source of the burning smell, so he disconnected his intercom and left his seat. At that moment it dawned on me that when he'd mentioned the fuel leak he'd been looking aft, and that when he saw fuel going past him on *his* starboard he had probably meant the port side of the aircraft. I looked immediately out to the port wing, just in time to see the small flap that covered the main tank filler cap pop open and a burst of whitish-orange flame quickly followed, engulfing the whole upper surface of the wing centre-section. I shouted to the navigator, somewhere behind me in the fuselage, to get back to his seat as I was going to ditch. Within seconds the side of the fuselage started to glow white, then burned with an intense white flame. The heat was almost unbearable. I had moved the gunsight to one side and was endeavouring to get the speed back as quickly as possible – until that moment we'd been belting at full throttle – whilst opening the top escape hatch. As the speed decreased the Beau became increasingly port wing heavy; obviously the result of damage to the port wing and, as I noticed later, the fact that the fabric had all burnt off the port elevator. Luckily the bank angle was about right for landing on the side of the fairly heavy swell.

As we hit the water the port mainplane broke away and, still burning, went over the top of the aircraft and landed in the sea to our starboard. Immediately on landing water streamed into the fuselage port side, putting out what flames were left, and the aircraft appeared to go under the water with the top hatch closing – and everything went dark and green. I undid my harness and parachute straps and pushed the escape hatch open with a great heave. As the sea gushed in I forced myself up through the opening, surprised to find myself in bright sunlight. The aircraft was still moving forward, nose down, at a fair speed and the sea was washing up over the nose. By then however it was sinking rapidly and I jumped over the leading edge of the starboard wing into the water as the front end started to disappear. I'd left my dinghy in the seat, still attached to my parachute, as the top escape hatch was too small to get through with them. However, I had my Mae West and I could swim – and more important than anything else at that moment was that I'd survived the flames and the ditching and was comparatively safe. I then tried to inflate my lifejacket by pulling on the small lever on the CO2 bottle at its base. Unfortunately for me, when the bottle had been attached, the fabric of the garment had been damaged, allowing all the contents of the bottle to escape into the water in a mass of bubbles. There was a tube attached to the Mae West so that it could be inflated by simply blowing into it, but this merely

created more bubbles. I was thus left treading water, wondering whether I could swim the 10 miles or so to the Turkish mainland, or whether I would have to swim the comple of miles back to Cos – an alternative I didn't relish at all.

Whilst considering these alternatives, I watched the Beau rapidly sinking. Then, as the rear part and the tail started to slide down into the depths, the rear canopy opened and the navigator seemed to pop out like a cork into the water. He didn't say anything but kept gesticulating to me, so I swam over to him and asked whether he had his dinghy. He nodded assent and pointed to his backside to indicate that it was still attached to his parachute harness. Whilst I was trying to unclip his dinghy I remembered the pigeon we carried in the aircraft for emergencies, which was in the nav's charge and kept in the rear of the fuselage. 'Did you bring the pigeon?' I asked. He then uttered his first words, ' – the pigeon. . .!' By this time, still less than a minute since we'd hit the water, the Beau had slid out of sight, but the port wing (or the fuel from it) was still burning on the water a little distance away. The nav had some burns on his hands and round the back of his neck between his helmet and the collar of his flying suit and appeared to be suffering from shock – who wasn't? With the dinghy inflated, we climbed into it and took stock of our situation, and sorted out the contents of the dinghy. There was a tube of violet ointment for burns, some chocolate, malt tablets and benzedrine

LINE-SHOOT. Flying Officer Alec Craig uses 'pilot's language' to explain a point to Flying Officer Pete Babury, 46 Squadron, Abu Sueir, Egypt. /Flt Lt E J Ledwidge, DFC

tablets. The latter we decided to partake of at once to keep our spirits up. After applying some of the violet ointment to the nav's burns and to some on my left arm and side, we looked towards the mainland. However, it was no longer in sight; due to our low position in the water the mainland was now over our horizon. The nav had a map with him and as the wind was from our starboard we would at least be drifted away from the German forces. Although it would not take us to the mainland, there were numerous islands to the north-east. With luck we should be able to land on one of these, so we planned how we could dry out our matches and cigarettes, light a fire and dry ourselves out. Cramped as it was, we decided to both remain in the dinghy for a while. The combined weight caused the whole dinghy to submerge to a depth of about two feet, so we were sitting upright with only our bodies from the chest and shoulders upward protruding from the water.

This decision proved to be a life-saver for us because soon after we'd settled down into the dinghy two Messerschmitt 109s flew low over the burning wing, and they would certainly have seen us if the bright yellow of our dinghy had been exposed on the surface. Several of these aircraft were flying around and appeared to be shooting at various targets on the water. (We learned afterwards that a number of individuals were escaping from the island, using small boats, supported by pieces of driftwood, paddling on improvised rafts, or even simply swimming towards the mainland about 10 miles away). We decided to sit tight, and although it was impossible to paddle with both of us in it we were definitely drifting in a north-easterly direction towards the other islands. As darkness came we saw the mosque-like building reappearing above the horizon – it was a lighthouse, with its light flashing regularly and getting brighter as the night progressed. Apart from taking more benzedrine tablets as soon as we began to feel tired, we'd discussed various things we might do on reaching terra firma, but my most vivid memory is of how we likened ourselves to the occupants of the 'pea-green boat'. Although at first neither of us could remember more than the first line or two of 'The Owl and the Pussycat', long before the end of our ordeal in the dinghy we were able to recite it from beginning to end!

Sometime after midnight we realised by reference to the flashing beacon on the lighthouse that the direction in which we were drifting had changed. We were now moving southwards at a fair rate of knots. So I got behind the dinghy and began to swim whilst the nav paddled, in an effort to maintain our heading towards the light against a now quite strong current. After some considerable time of such progress I was noticing hundreds of luminous mites glowing in the sea around me when,

suddenly, with a great woosh some monster leaped out of the water and almost turned the dinghy over. My immediate thought was 'sharks' and the next moment I was trying to get my legs out of the water. Luckily, there were a couple more swooshes nearby and they proved to be dolphins or porpoises travelling past us. As we neared the land we could hear the sea breaking on rocks some few hundred yards away, but the current around the headland was increasing, making it almost impossible to maintain our heading for the lighthouse. We had just about decided to abandon the dinghy and both try to swim for the headland when we suddenly ran into slack water and within moments my legs were touching bottom. We'd arrived on a shelf of rock, and waded ashore dragging the dinghy. We left the dinghy on the rocks at the base of some cliffs.

Finding a pathway up the cliffs we climbed up to the lighthouse, situated near the top, around which were clustered a number of small buildings, whilst below the actual tower was a large barn-like structure with big double doors. Inside this was a light and, looking through a gap between the fastened doors, we could see two men with a hurricane lantern. We attracted their attention and they came to the inside of the doors. All that we could say to them in Arabic (which we hoped they'd understand) was that we were 'Inglisi', but after repeating this several times between themselves they eventually enquired, 'Allemagne?'. We assured them we were not 'Allemagne' but 'Inglisi'. This exchange went on for quite some time until they seemed satisfied as to our identity and that we were not going to harm them in any way. They then came out of the barn and led us to a long low building next to a bungalow.

Inside was a large room with an open fireplace at one end nearest the door, whilst at the other end was a smaller room. We were extremely thirsty and were directed to the small room-cum-alcove wherein was a large earthenware pitcher of water and small jug which we used as a dipper. The water from that pitcher tasted like nectar after so long at sea, and I drank three or four jug-fulls before my thirst was quenched.'

Ledwidge and his navigator were then given a meal and a bed for the night, whilst their water-soaked clothing was dried. Next morning they were taken (by donkey . . .) to the village of Kefalka, where they boarded a boat which eventually took them to Bodrun, the centre for evacuating troops from Cos at that time. Here they learned that Sgt Holmes and Sgt Bell were in a hospital in the town, and next morning visited them briefly. Holmes, whom they'd last seen disappearing over the horizon with one engine of his Beau pouring smoke, told them that he'd covered about 20 miles when the engine stopped smoking – then gave up the ghost. He ditched and apart from some slight facial and head injuries, he and his navigator were intact. A third crew member in the same hospital was the late Wing Commander Reid's navigator, who was suffering from severe injuries after the CO's Beau spun from some 1,500 feet into the sea. Eventually, after a variety of adventures, Ledwidge and his companion arrived at Paphos, from where they were air-lifted to Egypt and Middle East headquarters for debriefing before rejoining 46 Squadron.

VETERAN. X7540 which first served with 68 Squadron; then became 'V-Victor' with 46 Squadron in 1943./*Crown copyright*

Last Op
VIC WEST

PASS-OVER. A merchant
vessel virtually disappears in
the cauldron of cannon fire and
RP strikes as a trio of Beaus
complete their onslaught.
/*Imperial War Museum*

Above: **BARRACK BLITZ. RP Beaus of the Balkan Air Force strafing a German headquarters building at Kalino, an island in the Dodencanese, early November 1944. The cordite trails from the rocket motors point the target with deadly accuracy.**/*British Official photo*

Allied Forces HQ had just issued a 'Special Order of the Day', and 272 Squadron, stationed at Falconara, 12 miles north of Ancona, had been ordered to knock out radar stations on the Yugoslav coast. April 10th, 1945 was a chilly Tuesday, and after leaving our tents we crossed the farm field to the mess tent for a breakfast of fried eggs bartered from the farmer (18 eggs for 10 cigarettes...). A quick ride to the ops room for the briefing – a simultaneous squadron strike on three radar stations, made up of three flights of four Beaus, escorted by Spitfires. It was to be a low-level approach across the Adriatic, observing W/T silence. My pilot, Les Fitton, and I, in F-Freddie were in the strike on Promontore Point, just south of the port of Pola. 'Crystal' and 'Black' Flights were to carry out strikes further up the coast towards Trieste. For me this meant very little in the way of pre-flight work, not much navigation detail, and no ground checks of W/T before take-off. The plan was to approach at low level (30 feet), cross the coast a few miles south of the target, fly inland about five miles, turn, climb to 1,000 feet and make the usual 20-degree diving attack in line astern, opening up with our cannons at 800 yards and firing eight 60lb HE RP in pairs of two. Then straight down to sea

level and back home having taken cine camera shots during the attack. The Spitfires were to follow us in with their cannons and add to the damage.

It was a short ride out to dispersal, the normal quick look round the aircraft, then climb aboard to stack my parachute and gear, and then the cockpit checks. I could see Les busy up front – I always left the armoured door open so that I could see what was going on; it gave me a sense of security being able to see him there, though I often wondered what I could do if anything ever happened to him. It took some time to clear the navigation table, lift it and scramble forward over the ammunition boxes. The sound of the starboard engine coming to life, followed by the port, really started it for me – that strange apprehensive feeling, a lightness in the stomach which soon went as we taxied out. No danger of overheating today, waiting for the USAF's Mitchells to land (they shared the strip with us). Out onto the runway where Les did his final checks. H – Hatch closed; Hydraulics OK – T – Trim for take-off; Throttle nut finger-tight – M – Mixture rich – P – Pitch fully fine – F – Fuel; Flaps set one-third for take-off – S – Set Gyro compass; Switches ON. 'You OK, Vic?' 'OK, Les'. A quick look to make sure he had closed the gills to one-third open, then oxygen mask on, brace legs and hands – the set take-off drill – 'Clear to take-off' over the R/T, then the characteristic sound of the Hercules engines as Les opened the throttles to Plus-4 Boost. Nudged the stick forward to get the tail wheel off the ground, followed a few seconds later by the lurch forward as the automatic boost came in. Would she swing this time? Yes, there came the jerk as Les used brakes and rudder to correct the bad habit of the Beau.

Airborne at 90 knots, undercarriage up, flaps closed, gills closed and we were over the sea. With the help of my forage cap I pulled back the cocking handle of the rear-facing Browning machine gun, then turned and reached forward to press the levers to 'load' the cannons, then set them to 'Fire' and warned Les. He turned on a northerly heading and fired a short burst to check them. Then, as the other Beaus completed their formalities, we formated. We on the starboard wing-tip of the leader Flt Lt Amos; Les Robins on our starboard tip, and No.2 over to port of the leader. Then down to sea level and off we set. The sea was calm and Les with the aid of the radio altimeter could maintain an accurate 30 ft height and concentrate on keeping station. I checked the compass and after a look through the drift recorder

checked on the track we were making. The two Spitfires alongside gave a satisfying sense of protection. A rude awakening came about two minutes before we reached the Yugoslav coast. Over the R/T came back-chat from a flight attacking a radar station to the north, and the numbing words, 'Crystal Leader has gone into the drink'. (This was Flt Lt P.C.T. Schaefer). Not much time for us to dwell on it fortunately as we crossed the coast and followed the attack plan.

We had climbed to 1,000 ft when the first black puffs appeared. A very short bit of straight and level, Les swung the pre-set gun-sight into position, then followed our leader at 220 knots into the dive. More heavy flak, then ominous streaks of tracer as the quadruple 20mm cannons opened up on us. Looking forward past Les's head I saw the explosions of the leader's rockets landing around the radar buildings, which soon became partially hidden in smoke and dust. Then the juddering racket as Les opened up with our cannons. How the Beau held together when all four of them fired always amazed me. As the fuselage filled with their smoke there came the *Bang, Sssh-Sssh* as the rockets went. There followed the drag of 'G' as Les pulled out of the dive, turning left to avoid any debris thrown up from the deck by our rockets, then straight down to sea level and off for home. Quiet congratulations on being safe so far were quickly interrupted by Les's query, 'Can you smell burning?' Panic...! A look forward, then out of the cupola at both engines – nothing seemingly wrong. Meanwhile Les had been busy and – relief!! – in the heat of the moment he had forgotten to switch off the cine camera, which had used up its film and was over-heating. Once out of range of the heavy flak, a turn onto north and the last few rounds through the cannons to set right the sometimes massive deviation on the compass caused by firing them. An uneventful trip home, full of chat and that wonderful feeling of relief when feet touched terra-firma. It transpired that our film of the attack showing RP explosions and cannon bursts (along with lots of sea and sky...) was the ONLY one. The leader forgot to switch his camera on, No.2 had a fault, and No.3 found the lens cover still on when he got back to base. Although we did not know it then, this was the last major operation carried out by 272 Squadron. Ten days later the Beaus were flown to Catania, Sicily, and the crews were dispersed, some returning to England, and some of us going to other units in the Far East theatre.

Above: **THE SHARP END. Head-on view of a Mk TFX, showing only too clearly the potential 'punch' of a Beau's war load – four 20mm cannons, six .303-inch machine guns, eight 3-inch rocket projectiles, and – though empty here – the torpedo crutches under the belly.**

'We Guard By Night'

RAY AVEYARD

NIGHT DEFENCE. X7898, 'G'
of 89 Squadron being prepared
for the evening's patrols, at a
forward dispersal on the
Mandalay Road, 1943.

Above: **INDIAN FIGHTER. Beau TFX, NE225, 'M' at dispersal under an Indian summer sky. The Observer's hand-fired machine gun here is an adapted .303-inch Browning gun.**

'The squadron came into being about August 1942 when personnel were posted to West Kirby, near Liverpool. At that time it was not known with which type of aircraft it was to be equipped. About August 28th we sailed from the Clyde and arrived in Capetown on September 25th. After about three weeks in a transit camp whilst decisions were being made at high level as to whether or not 176 Squadron was going to be required in the Middle East – this was around the time of El Alamein etc – the squadron journeyed up the African coast from Durban to Mombasa where there was further hanging around, but eventually we embarked for Bombay, arriving there at the end of November. The technical members of the unit were gathered together and again embarked on a Mecca pilgrim ship which dropped us off at Karachi. At Drigh Road airfield, in the Sind Desert, on the outskirts of Karachi, we were duly informed that we would be put to work assembling Vultee Vengeance dive bombers, as our own aircraft, which were to be Beaufighters, had yet to arrive. Although I was the signals NCO, because it appeared that I was the only member to have served with Beaus before (with 600 Squadron) I was made temporary stores officer. In January 1943 the whole squadron came together again at Dum Dum airport, Calcutta, where I was fully occupied at a new maintenance unit

(MU) and stores unit at Barrackpore. Here I identified Beau equipment being unloaded from ships on the Hooghli River, and got organised to see that 176 was the best-equipped Beau squadron in South East Asia. Later that month (15th) we received about five Beaufighters (nightfighters equipped with Mk VIII AI sets), flown in from Abu Sueir, Egypt by crews of 89 Squadron. These crews became the nucleus of 176 Squadron.

176 became operational immediately, responsible for the night defence of Calcutta, and were very soon in action on the same night, January 15th, when in brilliant moonlight Japanese aircraft made an attack on Calcutta. These were Army Type 97 bombers which were completely uncamouflaged and gleamed like silver fishes as they flew over in formation. The first Beau to sight the enemy (X7776, 'M') was piloted by Flight Sergeant A. M. Pring, who could hardly believe his eyes at the steady formation of 'silver fish'. After a careful look round, he closed in from the rear and shot down three Jap aircraft without receiving any return fire. The whole engagement lasted less than five minutes. This early success not only boosted squadron morale, but also the prestige of the RAF, and a civic reception was put on by the delighted residents of Calcutta. Pring was given an immediate award of a DFM, recommended for a commission, and was

in great demand as a guest at both private and civil dinner parties. One humourous incident which occurred at Dum Dum was the occasion when it was decided to 'scramble' the Beaus. The aircrews on 'immediate readiness' dashed out to the dispersal but found the aircraft guarded by Sikhs who would not let *anyone* near the aircraft until the proper password was given! Of course, we didn't know it, so some 10 minutes were wasted whilst the password was obtained, and only then could the crews scramble in, start engines and take off.

We remained at Dum Dum for about two months and then moved to a newly-completed airfield at Baigachi, approximately 40 miles outside Calcutta on the Jessore road. We stayed here for some time and the only incident outstanding in my memory was a daylight raid made on Calcutta on December 6th, 1943. The attack was made by medium bombers, this time escorted by Zero fighters. On this particular day, round about mid-day, a Spitfire squadron had just flown into Dum Dum after making the long flight from Palam, Delhi. Although the Spitfire CO was requested to scramble his aircraft to meet the attack, he (rightly, I think) refused, saying his pilots were fatigued and in no fit condition to go straight into action. It was decided therefore to put up the one flight of 176 Squadron's nightfighter Hurricanes. Pring, now com-

missioned, just happened to be at dispersal at the time and, though not officially on duty, requested permission to fly one of the Hurricanes, and took off with the others. (These particular Hurricanes were fitted with four 20mm cannon and pilot-operated Mk VI AI gear). The Japanese bombers were reported by Calcutta GCI Station to be at about 18,000 feet, but no mention was made of the fighter cover. The Hurricanes were vectored onto the Japs and dived towards them, only to be jumped by Zeros. Pilot Officer Pring was hit and went straight into the ground from 20,000 feet. At Baigachi our Beaufighters were scrambled but were considered too valuable to be committed to daylight combat, so were sent away from the area until the raid was over. With the loss of the Hurricanes, replacement Beaus were sent in to bring 176 up to strength again; thus for a spell we were only involved in training and familiarisation flying, with a few patrols off the Andaman Islands and the Chittagong area of Assam.

176 Squadron had at that time a very experienced ex-airline pilot as its commander, Wg Cdr Henry Goddard, who was very keen for the squadron to be active. He was, however, promoted to Group Captain of (I think) 221 Wing and, using his influence, was able to have one detached flight sent to Imphal in northern Assam. Ground crews were flown to

Right: **GROUND STRAFE.** Low-level attack on enemy-occupied Lashio airfield by Sqn Ldr Hunt, B Flight commander in 177 Sqn, 1944. Targets are the Japanese 'Zero' fighters in their individual disperal pens. In a subsequent reconnaissance it was found that no damage had been done to the aircraft! */W G Herr*

Below: **Pilot Officer Arthur Maurice Owen Pring, DFM** who achieved wide publicity for destroying three Japanese 'Sally' bombers over Calcutta on the night of January 15th, 1943, whilst serving with 176 Squadron. He had previously seen operational service with 604, 125 and 89 Squadrons, and scored at least six victories prior to his 'hat-trick'. Awarded a DFM for this feat, and commissioned from Flight Sergeant in May 1943, he was killed in action on December 6th, 1943./*Indian Official*

Imphal in a DC3 flown by an American crew, and when we arrived over the Imphal valley (which was 27 miles long and nine miles wide) one of the Americans came back to ask us if we knew which strip we were going to. None of us knew and we flew low over one strip at the southern end of the valley, known as Wangjin. Puffs of smoke from the ground told us we were being fired upon, and we heard later that the Japs were at one end of this strip and our army at the other end. The Americans finally landed at the only all-weather strip at Imphal, only to be re-directed to another rolled paddy field not far away called Tulihull. We were met by Grp Capt Goddard who said, 'The climate is healthy and the natives are friendly...' Naturally, the move was supposed to have been secret, but after five Beaufighters landed and had taxied under the trees, the jungle parted and there was the inevitable char wallah with his can of hot tea and his tin box full of sticky iced cakes!

The detachment's mandate at Imphal was to fly 'rhubarbs' (low-level sweeps) into Burma at night looking for targets such as water craft moving on the Chindwin River, or for any road and rail traffic. Anything seen was to be attacked. At this time we had Indian Army or West African troops looking after the perimeter

patrols, and our domestic site was what was known as a 'box'. This meant that earth had been piled up on four sides of a square with only one opening to enter and leave by. We lived in tents within the box and foxholes were dug adjacent to each tent. Occasionally the Japs would infiltrate during the night and send mortar bombs in our general direction, until the army rushed up with jeep-drawn 40-pounder guns or other mortars to return the fire. When such attacks were known to be a possibility we frequently had to move at half an hour's notice to another strip, Kangla, a few miles north and just south of the famous Kohima Box. Whilst at Imphal we were attacked by Japanese aircraft. One daylight strafing attack on Tulihull was memorable because several chaps were at the time perched precariously on a single bamboo pole over the ditch which served as our communal latrine. It needs little imagination to know where they ended up! (They all emerged safely, but were without friends for several days afterwards . . .)

The squadron gave cover when Orde Wingate's Chindits were dropped into selected spots in central Burma, and continued to carry out its patrols, slowly increasing its destruction of river craft, road transports and trains. One small diversion was the finding (yes, *finding*) a long-nosed Blenheim IV bomber which had been left behind, heavily camouflaged, in the 1942 retreat from Burma. This was given a top overhaul and Grp Capt Goddard himself came down to Kangla to take the Blenheim up on its first test flight. He got off OK but only made a hurried circuit during which we saw the pilot's top sliding hatch cover fly off and flutter to the ground, and then quickly landed. Immediately on stopping, the group captain leapt out, tearing his jacket off and beating his body with his hands. Apparently an ants' nest had been behind the blind flying panel and had been blown around the cockpit immediately on take-off. Later a volunteer patrol crossed the Manipur river into 'no man's land' and recovered the hatch cover, and this Blenheim – loaded with four 250lb bombs and volunteer crews (sometimes drawn from the ground staff) – was subsequently flown many times by the group captain, and I believe had at least one bridge destroyed to its credit.

176 Squadron also provided other small detachments to Chittagong, and later Akyab and Ramree Islands as the Japanese were gradually pushed back. During this period one of our Beaus from Chittagong shot down an American

Flying Fortress which failed to answer a Very Light challenge when returning from a bombing mission. Fortunately all the American crew were able to bail out and were all safely returned to their unit. However, on hearing that the Beau had used only *four* rounds from each cannon, they insisted on giving a party for the Beau crew – they just didn't believe that one of their Fortresses could be shot down so easily. Imphal, which at one time was surrounded by three Jap divisions, was finally relieved after ground troops broke through near Kohima, and one night we were all brought to our feet by the sounds of tanks advancing down the Tiddim road. A few weeks later he returned to our base at Baigachi; our only casualties of the long detachment being one Beau and its crew. This aircraft flew into a hillside near Kangla, killing both crew members, and it was a very sad memorial service that our detachment attended alongside the Manipur road where the remains of our friends were buried.

With the start of the Japanese retreat in Burma, the next area to be looked at was Malaya and planning commenced for its invasion. 176 was moved from Baigachi down to Ceylon where we had short spells on the 'dromes at Vavuniya and Ratmalana (Columbo), finally going to Minneriya, which we shared with an Australian Liberator squadron and a Fleet Air Arm unit flying Barracudas. Operationally, things were now quiet. Exercises were carried out with the Royal Navy, and indeed our CO (Sqn Ldr Welch, I think) did a practice landing in a Beaufighter onto an aircraft carrier – though he wasn't too keen on this particular operation. With the dropping of the two atom bombs on Japan the war finished, so Malaya was never invaded from Ceylon. 176 moved back to Baigachi where, on June 1st, 1946 and not long after being re-equipped with Mosquito aircraft, formal disbandment of the squadron took place. Lots of useful equipment which had been 'won' during the period when the squadron was a going concern all had to be ditched quite literally in a hole in the ground, as it was 'not on official unit inventory'. 176 Squadron, whose official unit motto, '*We guard by Night*' is the heading for these reminiscences, was a unit with plenty of potential, but because of the nature of the Burma war zone, resulting necessarily in continual splitting into various detachments operating individually, it never quite achieved the normal splendid cohesion of a complete unit under fire together.'

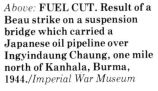

Above: FUEL CUT. Result of a Beau strike on a suspension bridge which carried a Japanese oil pipeline over Ingyindaung Chaung, one mile north of Kanhala, Burma, 1944./*Imperial War Museum*

Centre left: COMING HOME. A Beau VIF, 'X', about to land on its base airstrip, Burma, 1944. /*Imperial War Museum*

Bottom left: Flying Officer Charles Basil Crombie, an Australian serving with 176 Squadron, with Warrant Officer R C Moss as his Observer, tackled a Japanese bomber formation onver Budge Budge (south of Calcutta) on the night of January 19th, 1943. His Beau was hit and set ablaze during his initial attack but he remained in his seat, destroyed two and seriously damaged a third bomber before the Beau's fuel tanks exploded and he was forced to take to his parachute. He had previously served with 25 and 89 Squadrons, and by 1945 was a Sqn Ldr, DSO, DFC, but was killed in a flying accident on August 26th, 1945. He is talking here with Wg Cdr J A O'Neill, DFC, commander of 176 Squadron at that time. /*Indian Official*

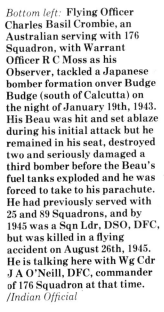

87

Flying Elephants

BRIAN HARTNESS

LOCO-BUSTERS – the nickname given at one period to 27 Squadron because of its prodigious score of rail locomotives destroyed. A typical train-strike is illustrated here; Flt Lt Williams and Flt Sgt Fosh in Beas 'H' and 'G' attacking the Japanese railway along the Kume Road on September 23rd, 1943./*Sqn Ldr E S Welch*

Above: **EAST OF THE BRAHMAPUTRA.** RD367, 'H' of 27 Squadron in August 1945 beating low over the Burman plains. Contemporary SEAC (South East Asia Command) livery – white bands on both wings and tail – is clearly evident here; also the tasteful outlining of the individual aircraft letter./*D A F Jackson*

Above right: **DUMBO** – the insigne painted on the nose of NE807, 'F' of 27 Squadron in October 1945./*K Jarvis*

Below right: **WEARY WILLIE** – Beau TFX KW393, 'W' another of 27 Squadron's aircraft in early 1945. In October 1944 this machine was coded 'G' with the same unit./*D A F Jackson*

By the autumn of 1942 the Allied forces in India were gathering strength for a long struggle to regain the offensive against the Japanese. In North Africa the turn of the tide of battle in favour of the Allies was sufficiently successful to permit a long overdue flow of reinforcement supplies, particularly aircraft, to be sent to the 'Forgotten War' in India and Burma. One of the fresh designs allotted to India was the mighty Beaufighter. Apart from some early deliveries of Mk 1 Beaus, the majority of Beaus sent to the Far East initially were Mk VI's. With its accent on rating for low-level performance the Beau Mk VI was probably the nearest approach to an ideal aeroplane that could have been chosen for the role of what is now termed interdiction. And it was in Burma that the Beaufighter acquired its legendary nickname, 'Whispering Death' – a soubriquet which, despite the many versions of its origin published in the past, actually originated as the whimsy of an RAF officers' Mess in India. The nickname quickly became universally accepted as the most apt description of the particularly 'silent' approach of a Beau to any target. This peculiar characteristic proved shattering to Japanese troops' morale – retribution from the skies delivered without warning and a terrifying suddenness. Just two examples of a Beau's ability to reach an objective unheralded illustrate its effect. A single Beaufighter on a free-lance sweep spotted a full-dress ceremonial parade of Japanese at Myitkyina, the largest enemy air base in north Burma at the time. The occasion was in honour of Emperor

Hirohito's birthday, and troops were drawn up in a hollow square round the main flagpole, about to salute the Rising Sun ensign. The Beau made just two passes, killing a high proportion of the parade, and with one burst severing the flagpole and draping the ensign over the bodies of its colour guard. Another Beau strafed the training centre for officers of the traitor Burmese army at Pyinmana – slaughtering dozens of men caught totally unprepared on an open parade ground.

The first Beaufighter to reach India was the initial aircraft issued to 27 Squadron, re-formed at Amarda Road airfield in September 1942. This Beau arrived on October 22nd, to be followed by two more aircraft on November 18th. By mid-December 1942, 27 Squadron had 13 Beaufighters on strength, and at Christmas, led by Wg Cdr Harry Daish, 27's commander, a trio of 27's Beaus made the first-ever operational sortie in the Far East theatre. One of those pilots was Brian Hartness, then a sergeant. For the remainder of the Burma campaign Beaufighters, though never in great numbers, fought a vital 'backwoods' war, seeking out Japanese transport and installations and spreading a reign of terror over the enemy. 27 Squadron, nicknamed 'The Flying Elephants' after the elephant motif of the unit's official badge, pioneered the Beaufighter in Burma (as indeed it pioneered the use of the DH Mosquito later). The following extracts of individual sorties flown by Brian Hartness have been selected from an unpublished manuscript in which he describes his flying career. Though one

man's particular experiences, they represent thousands of similar sorties and incidents experienced by Burma Beau crews.

'The date was February 13th, 1943 – an ominous date. Not so unlucky, but it might have been. Even at Agartala (27's base) an attack on Toungoo airfield meant that we must refuel at a forward airstrip in the paddy fields known as Ramu. The procedure was the same as the Christmas Day attack – fly to the south of the airfield, make one attack, then shoot up anything that offered itself on the way home. With 'Snowy' Swift leading, our two Beaus hurdled the Yomas, keeping as close to the ground as we dared. We crossed the Irrawaddy; my navigator, Jack Shortis, remarking that he thought we were too far north. This was surprising as Snowy's navigator was very experienced. We hit the railway line, went into full power and turned north. After 20 minutes with the taps full on there was no sign of Toungoo. Snowy realised this and was about to turn south when we saw a railway train ahead. Snowy elected to attack it, making our first mistake. We destroyed the locomotive in a cloud of steam, but it warned the Japs that we were around. We then flew south along the railway which meant that we'd have to make an about-turn when we attacked Toungoo. There was a satellite strip to the north of the main airfield and as we crossed it I saw several Zero fighters – if they got off in time, I thought, we were for it. I was flying on Snowy's port side.

As we pulled up I saw an Army 97 bomber just taxying into its dispersal. It was a perfect target and I dived at it, giving it my full fire power. The Japs round it ran like mad and I watched my cannon shells hit it. It blew up in a most spectacular manner. I continued my dive as low as I dared, cleared the airfield amidst puffs of bursting ack-ack, then began a low turn to the north. Out of the corner of my eye I saw Snowy flying back over the airfield surrounded by flak bursts. Then I was over the satellite again and I fired at an Oscar in its dispersal pen, but had used up all my cannon ammunition attacking the train and the Army 97. I saw the Browning .303 bullets hit the Oscar but it didn't blow up, so I claimed it later as damaged. At that moment Jack shouted to me that we were

Top: **FIRST IN INDIA.** Trio of 27 Squadron Beaus sweeping across the Burma border, 1943. 27 was the first unit to receive and operate Beaufighters in the Far East campaign area, flying its first operations in December 1942.

Above: **BEAUS OVER BURMA.** Neat Vic of 27 Squadron's Beaus in 1945 nearest, 'H' being RD367. */D A F Jackson*

being fired at. I was very low at the time and foolishly took my eyes off the direct line of flight. A stream of tracer bullets were coming from a machine gun post on the ground. I jinked the aircraft violently and those few seconds of inattention to direction were enough.

A particular hazard of low flying in Burma was the number of teak stumps left standing after being 'killed' so that they might season. They were high enough to be a real danger, and to my horror I saw that I was too close to one of them to avoid it. I hit it fair and square. It smashed in the leading edge of my starboard wing between the fuselage and the engine nacelle, and severely dented the exhaust collector ring which formed the front cowling of the engine. By some miracle the propeller was undamaged. I

cannot remember the thoughts that went through my head in those few terrifying seconds, but I well remember the relief at finding the Beau still flying on serenely. I told Jack what had happened. His reply was one of admonishment. His main concern was the fact that I had also ripped the IFF aerial from its moorings. The IFF set was our means of letting our radar know we were 'friendly', and Jack was firmly convinced that we would be shot down by some trigger-happy fighter boy. By this time I'd lost sight of Snowy and deciding that I had had enough for one day I headed for the Yomas and the long climb home. Collecting myself together, I made a check round all the instruments and found everything normal; but our time spent at full throttle had played hell with the fuel state. I told Jack that we would go back to Ramu and take on some fuel (we'd been briefed to return straight to Agartala).

We reached Ramu safely and I made a very careful approach and landing due to the damage to my Beau (EL286), but she behaved perfectly. The ground staff at Ramu were in doubt about my taking off again in a bent aeroplane, but I insisted because there were no repair facilities there. At Agartala we found that Snowy had arrived back an hour previously, convinced that the burning aircraft at Toungoo was me. Everyone was pleased that I'd done some severe damage to the Japs, but Sqn Ldr Illingworth had a quiet word with me about the damage to EL286. I'm afraid I didn't take the criticism too well, but for me the final straw came when Snowy upbraided me

for not following him back over the airfield at Toungoo. I told him quite plainly that I was never in a position to do that without presenting myself as an Aunt Sally to the Jap ack-ack. To his great credit, he took my fiery outburst quite calmly even though I had overstepped the mark in my language to a senior officer. However, I'll never forget the remark made by my Scottish corporal, in charge of EL286's ground crew. When I apologised for bending the kite, he merely said, 'Forget it', and turned to the other Scots saying, 'There I told ye, oor pilot will always come back' – an accurate prophecy for which I will always be grateful.'

Brian Hartness completed a further 23 sorties, and at the beginning of 1944 flew

his penultimate, and 26th, operational trip with the 'Flying Elephants'. It was a night 'rhubarb' – a type of operation in which 27 Squadron excelled by then.

'On January 3rd, 1944, two of us received instructions to report to the briefing room. The OC Agartala Wing told us that 224 Group had detailed an attack on Heho airfield, but he was not happy about it. He rang Operations and told them that he considered this sortie to be too dangerous because Heho lay in an area surrounded by hills. Group gave him permission to make his own choice. He briefed me to patrol the railway south from Mandalay to Thazi Junction, then westwards to Myingyan. The Thazi – Myingyan railway ran close to the Jap airfield at Meiktila and we were told to

divert around it. He sent the other aircraft further south. It was half moonlight and the Burmese plain stood out quite clearly – it was a beautiful night for our operations. There was a desultory burst of ack-ack at Madalay but it was very inaccurate. I flew along the railway without sighting anything until I arrived at Thazi. I sighted some headlights from road transport running into Thazi from the east. Getting myself into position, I dived at them and pressed the trigger. Nothing happened – I'd forgotten to turn the safety catch to 'Fire'.

By the time I came round into position again the transport had heard me and dowsed its lights. Then some ack-ack fire got a little too close and I turned away towards Myingyan. Again there was nothing to be seen. I was beginning to think that it would be an abortive sortie, and had just about reached the point where I was to divert to avoid Meiktila, when I saw the sudden glow of a locomotive firebox being opened. This time I remembered to turn the safety catch, sighted the guns on that open firebox and fired. As I pulled up from the attack I saw the train of tankers underneath, a gusher of steam issuing forth from the locomotive. I came round again and fired at the tankers, two of which went up with a glorious bang. I broke away to the right, intending to make another attack; then I saw the broad expanse of a runway underneath – I was right over Meiktila! All hell seemed to be let loose. Tracers came at me from all directions and I crammed on full power, corkscrewing the Beau violently. I felt a

slight jolt and wondered if we had been hit, but the Beau flew on. The firework display ceased once I was clear of Meiktila. Thinking we had had sufficient war for one night, I nevertheless continued along the railway to Myingyan without sighting anything more. As I crossed the Irrawaddy I put the power to full climb and began the journey home – but our troubles were far from over.

I had reached about 8,000 feet, crossing over that 4,000 ft range of hills that preceded the main range when the port engine coughed and the throttle banged shut. I quickly corrected the inevitable swing to port. Pete Dilworth, my navigator, came up on the intercomm, 'What's wrong, Brian?' I told him that our port engine had cut out. It was a moment for decision. I gingerly opened the port throttle and the engine picked up. A looked round the gauges showed everything normal. Now what to do? I checked our fuel supply and it told me that a long flight to the south and over the hills at their low point was out of the question. I took a quick look at my map, saw that I could make Imphal without having to exceed 4,000 feet. But that presented another difficulty because Imphal was in a valley surrounded by high hills. I had landed there in daylight and thought at the time that it was a dangerous place. And I might have to fly around whilst they laid out a flare path. But I saw no alternative. The engine was still giving power so I decided to keep climbing as best as I could. I told Pete to give me a course for Imphal and suggested he try to raise Agartala on the W/T,

telling them that we were in trouble. I altered course as soon as Pete came up with it and continued climbing. I refrained from putting the engines into 'S' gear and hoped that we could get maximum height without doing this. Pete rattled away with the Morse key but got no reply from Agartala. (They heard him, but he didn't receive their reply).

The engines continued to run sweetly and we had reached 18,000 feet with our oxygen supply full on. Then I had second thoughts. I told Pete that everything seemed normal and did he agree that we should take a chance on crossing the mountains. His answer was prompt, 'If you think it's all right, let's have a go.' I turned westwards, telling him that we'd sort out a course for Agartala when we had crossed over. Right over the middle of those damn mountains the engine coughed again. Again, I opened the throttle very carefully and she picked up. I flew with one hand on the control column, the other holding the throttle open. I called up Agartala on the R/T and got an immediate reply, quite clear, at what must have been about 150 miles distant. They told me they'd received our W/T transmission and asked how things were going. They had contacted Imphal and laid on a flare path. I told them what I was doing, they came up with a bearing, and I turned onto it. Calling them every five minutes reporting progress, and as the mountains faded away behind me, I eased the throttles back and began a descent. Then Agartala's beacon came into view. I was still at 8,000 feet and circled the airfield, gently reducing

height. I didn't want to close the throttles too much in case that port engine failed again.

I made a fairly high approach to the runway and, when I gauged that we were within gliding distance of the runway, closed the throttles, praying that I wouldn't overshoot and have to go round again. Touching down in a three-pointer at the third flare, I brought the Beau to a standstill at the last one. I taxied to the marshalling point and switched off. I found myself bathed in sweat. The OC Wing had waited up for us and congratulated me on the night's work, laughing off my failure to turn on my guns at Thazi. The other Beau had returned half an hour before, having seen nothing at all. I can perhaps be excused for feeling pleased with myself, but I hoped I'd never have such heart-stopping moments again. A subsequent inspection of the Beau (JL767, 'A') revealed that the cause of the misfires was a loose adaptor in the ignition system. But I still wonder what made that throttle kick back.'

95

Burma Nav

EDGAR WELCH

TON-UP TEAM. Flight Sergeant Ron Thorogood, pilot, (right) and his Observer, Fg Off Edgar Welch, who were responsible for destroying 27 Squadron's 100th locomotive in October 1943. They are examining a belt of 20mm cannon shells./*Imperial War Museum*

Before we met at Catfoss OTU, my pilot, Ron Thorogood, had been trained at various places, including Canada; whereas all my training was in the UK, finishing at Squires Gate, near Blackpool, on what was firmly a Coastal Command course in anticipation of Beaus being used for long range convoy cover. The result of this was that we got to the 'starting line' with morale sustained (at a period of unbroken defeats) and the prospect of a worthwhile job – with none of the misgivings of some of the top-heavy bomber crews. God's providence and arithmetic apart, it should be appreciated that to complete 30 successful operations together a crew of two had to be complementary and reasonably complete, and on long range operations under no need to ask any guidance from anyone. In our OTU exercises Ron and I were happy to discover this firm basis in ourselves. Ron had some reassurance from my mechanical and electrical know-how, and ability to fly an aircraft (in the air). He, on the other hand, I found to be an excellent navigator with a sound instinct for direction.

Mention must now be made of the most important Beau point for the navigator – his limited vision from his cupola 18 feet behind the pilot, who sat well up in the nose. In a steep approach to an actual cannon attack the navigator could see everything very well. In a long cross-country run, however, there was a deficiency because in level flight the nav could only see two-thirds of the ground – the wings and engines were in the way – and had to depend on his pilot for the front third. It was often best on operations to do most of the approach flight of up to 600 miles with the navigator looking backwards with his seat reversed. That way he got a good look at an expected landmark, though the Beau would be past it. He could, of course, walk forward and stand behind the pilot, but this left rear visibility uncovered and was not a good idea.

In Burma the navigation was mostly dead reckoning, with none of the electronic aids used in Europe, and not difficult once it had been appreciated that the compasses would have considerable error after the cannons had been fired – as the result of some magnetic effect. Winds and weather tended to be settled for weeks at a time and over large areas, except during early monsoon periods when it could become quite suddenly violent with thunderous lowering clouds and air strips awash. In our own territory there had to be radio watch

and, when returning in the dark, radio checks for bearings etc. Out of our territory there had to be a non-stop look-out for strange aircraft – Japs *or* Americans. The latter became so unpredictable that eventually we had an arrangement under which they operated in the morning and we in the afternoon/ evening – and they *still* managed to shoot down two of our Beaus into the Akyab swamps... Approaching the target the guns and camera had to be set ready, and a check made that the right petrol tanks were in use – preferably the wing inners. In actual attacks pilots tended to become engrossed in their cannon shooting and temporarily ignored the world outside the aiming ring. In brief, pilot and navigator had non-stop activity and co-operation. This all, I think, tended to maintain a calm atmosphere and a satisfactory feeling at the day's end – however exhausting – and a desire for settled crews to stick together. The Beau was an exceptionally quiet, comfortable and reliable aircraft, and we never had mechanical trouble.

November 14th, 1943
In company with Fg Off 'Ginger' Hassell and his navigator, Flt Sgt Thomas, Ron Thorogood and I were to make attacks in the Prome area on the Irrawaddy. They were in A Flight and we were in B Flight. The flights usually operated quite separately, in friendly rivalry – maybe as 'policy' – and this was a first effort at cooperation, perhaps in the hope that we had something to learn from each other. It was to be a night take-off, so the evening before I went to bed early. All briefing had been done in the afternoon and the maps marked up. At two in the morning the guard came round to rouse us and lighted the hurricane lamp. I pulled on my carefully equipped jungle suit, heavy boots and gun, and stumbled off across the pitch-dark compound to meet the others, sleepy in the cool starlight, drinking coffee. Then into the truck, with Ginger driving – the CO of No 27 Squadron (Wg Cdr Nicolson, VC) waved as we went past his verandah – onto the jungle road down to the air strip. It was a beautiful night and we were at peace with the world – though privately maybe we hoped there would be no delay, because in delay, however well-intentioned, there is a smell of danger. But all was ready when we arrived – two Beaus dimlighted against the protective sand bank with the ground crews waiting to help us in. Final check over and then the clattering roar of our motors. Straight out onto the runway,

marked with oily glim lamps (we never got round to electricity at Agartala), then skimming along like two great bats, sweeping into the air and formating steadily for the south. We could see Ginger's Beau (JL535, 'J') ghostlike against the sky.

The Beau had armour doors in the bulkhead behind the pilot, designed by a mind aiming at the futility of absolute safety instead of relative safety. The better bet was for a clear view from me to Ron up front, so we always had the doors fixed open. We chatted and had a biscuit, with an eye on the compass and my chart – a steady 210 mph, and the night wore through to dawn to find us dead on track – high over the mountains and deep down the Irrawaddy into enemy country; a lovely sunrise driving away the valley mist. We were not thinking of anything special, in fact as we opened the throttles and tore down to the Jap aerodrome at the river crossing maybe we were a little too carefree, and didn't sidle down the mountain shadows as we might have done. Ginger swept magnificent across the river and we, probably scenting trouble, got down close to the water – and then we saw it all happen – a shadow in the sun.

Top: **ECHELON.** Three of 27 Squadron's Beaus in tight formation heading out over Burma on a daylight sweep, 1943. After the first few months of operations it was deemed more practical to despatch pairs, or only single Beaus on patrols, thus assisting surprise tactics.

Above: **TRAIN IN THE TOILS.** Japanese rail train being shot up at Shwebo on February 2nd, 1944 by Beau 'K' of 27 Squadron.

Left: Flying Officer Edgar Welch (right) and Ron Thorogood (hidden from view) receive the congratulations of Flight Sergeant George Salter, BEM and the rest of 27 Squadron's B Flight erks on October 20th, 1943 at Agartala airfield – the sortie on which the unit's 100th Japanese locomotive victim was chalked up./*Sqn Ldr E S Welch*

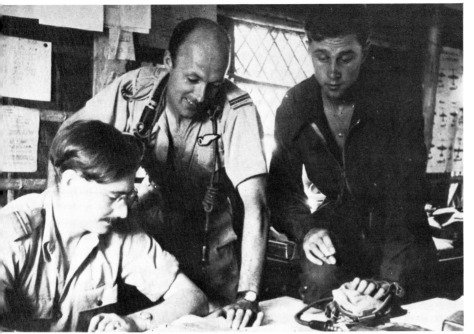

The Japs had seen Ginger's aircraft silhouetted against the western mist and held their fire until he turned to attack the 'drome, then caught him on the turn with a streaking blue-smoked barrage. His Beau wobbled and then turned down the river, heavily – back over the western bank – and then started to climb, labouring, with a trail of blue-black smoke pouring from its starboard engine. We flew on clear round the aerodrome and then turned back, climbing to escort the battered Beau and help if we could. The mountain ridge here was only 5,000 feet and Ginger soon had her up to 3,000 – then we saw the starboard motor stop and the smoke tail away, oil finished perhaps and she hadn't caught fire. He didn't seem to be nursing the Beau on the remaining motor or have any hope of slanting his flight to labour over the ridge down to the comparative safety of the distant sea shore and the Arakan sands. He just drove straight towards the mountains – getting closer – and we entered a longside valley.

On the remaining motor Ginger was hardly maintaining height and then that too started to smoke. We flew up close and called on the R/T for them to jump, but there was no response or even a sign – they just seemed to be sitting there, looking ahead. I once saw a Beau with 72 holes in it return safely, but I reckon this one had taken too much. We pulled up over the crest and looked back as the great pillar of fire leapt up. One stunned sweep round the holocaust and then we dived south for the remaining 100 miles of our attacks on road, river and rail. We had finally just blown a Jap army lorry off a road when something smacked against my boot and I saw stars and felt blood soak through my sock. A split Jap explosive bullet lay against the cannon breech. We turned for home – and it was still only the first brightness of the morning.

December 16th, 1943 – our longest day.
Ron and I took off at 0835 hours in Beau Y-Yorker on an offensive recce down the Sandaway coast to the Jap aerodrome at Gwa, returning over Ramree Island where we were to photograph defences being prepared by the Japs in expectation of an Allied landing. It was to be our 25th operation. In company with Fg Off Dave Innes (an Australian pilot) and his regular navigator Fg Off Paddy Stirling, we left Agartala and drove south along the coast (with a diversion along Taungup Pass). The trip was uneventful but exceptionally hot down near the sea, and as

Left: **GREEN ENDORSEMENT.** Beau 'Y', 27 Squadron, which was hit by flak over Gwa on December 16th, 1943. Its pilot, Ron Thorogood, completed his recce, then overflew the squadron's base, Agartala, and belly-landed at the nearest Maintenenace Unit, Kanchrapara. His skilful handling that day earned him a Green Endorsement in his log book./*Sqn Ldr E S Welch*

Below: **RUN-UP.** A typical Beau strike – Japanese river steamer at Pakokku in the process of being blasted by Beau 'M', 27 Squadron, on December 10th, 1943. Cannon fire is registering centrally, while nearer splashes are the cross-over machine gun 'sighter' bullets./*Sqn Ldr E S Welch*

we swished over Gwa aerodrome we were sitting in a pool of sweat with shirt, parachute harness and Mae West pushed back off the shoulders over the seat back. The aerodrome looked deserted until we put a blast into one of the buildings – held too long perhaps – and there was an immediate response, hitting us under the port engine and producing a blue-grey trail.

First thing to do was to give Ron the shortest course to the north for home, then shuffle on Mae West etc. Then the trail of 'smoke' tailed off and we realised it was only from the port undercarriage hydraulic fluid. All engine oil pressures were OK, so our sweat subsided and we had a bite of lunch. Continuing north we turned east at Ramree to do our photographic circuit over tank traps et al and then set course for Agartala base. Arriving there it was soon apparent that the undercarriage was jammed up, so we continued to the reserve maintenance depot at Kanchrapara, near Calcutta, and landed wheels-up on the grass, with bent propellers as the only other damage. So far, so good, though we'd been in the air over seven hours and were exhausted. Ron had the bright eyes of fever and, it later transpired, was already well on into a bout of malaria. But our day still had a long way to go.

Kanchrapara was actually the maintenance depot for the Bengal Nagpur Railway, and the RAF facilities were incidental. The senior railway executives were important people and lived in considerable splendour with ready hospitality, against a background of soft

candlelight on a great mahogany dining table set with silver. We were delighted therefore when the duty officer who had to deal with our damaged Beau reported that the 'big house' had invited us to dinner and to stay there overnight. He then proceeded to fire his Very Light pistol, which was his arrangement to call up the duty truck, to take us along. Unfortunately the glowing light after shooting up high came down smack on the thatched roof of the canopy covering the airstrip's fire engine – and set all ablaze. With difficulty we got the duty officer on a ladder up to the roof and started a line of water buckets to dowse the fire. This worked well enough until just when I was handing up two full buckets of water he flung down an empty – which gashed my head. I now looked as if I really had been in the wars, but not enough to spoil the hospitality and a glimpse of the British 'Raj' as it used to be. This was indeed our longest day.'

Top left: **DE-BRIEFING.** Flt Sgt Ron Thorogood (rt) and Fg Off Edgar Welch (centre) reporting to the 27 Sqn Intelligence Officer, Pilot Officer Blackburn-Daniell at Agartala, October 20th, 1943. /*Sqn Ldr E S Welch*

Bottom left: 'Attacked from north-east in U-Uncle; our first burst blew off camouflage and set it ablaze' – a graphic extract from the report by Ron Thorogood and Edgar Welch, 27 Sqn, describing their destruction of a half-million gallon oil storage tank near Padigon on September 11th, 1943./*Sqn Ldr E S Welch*

101

SALVO. Beau X, NE543, UB-E
of 455 Squadron RAAF
releasing a broadside of 3-inch
RP over the Bay of Biscay.
/Imperial War Museum

A Beau's Caress

Far left top: **TOTE THAT BARGE** . . . Armourers carrying an RP with 60lb HE head to Beau NE646, 'V' in Burma, 1944. The main 'body' of an RP was simply a steel tube containing the rocket's propellant; a single 11lb stick of cordite in cruciform section with its electrically-ignited initiation in situ. A variety of war or practice heads could be threaded into the forward end of the rocket motor, and at the rear were four slots to receive guidance fins. Attachment to the wing rails was by use of metal saddles./*Imperial War Museum*

Top left: Once the saddles were attached to the RP, the next step was sliding each rocket onto its rail. Here armourers are loading Beau '2-G' of 404 Squadron RCAF in May 1944. The RP heads illustrated were 25lb SAP (Semi-Armour Piercing) Shot – an anti-shipping head./*British Official*

Bottom left: **FEEDING THE CANNON.** Armourers threading in a belt of 20mm shells to Beau V8748, ZJ-R of 96 Squadron, Drem, Scotland, October 1943. A posed scene specially for the Press. Beaus could carry up to 240 shells per cannon./*Imperial War Museum*

Top right: **SOUND AND FURY.** Ear protection was necessary when a Beau's cannons 'spoke' . . . A8-122 of 93 Squadron RAAF, (SK-R) having its cannons tested at the stop butts after major servicing./*L Mutton*

Centre right: **ROCKET TRAILS.** An RAAF Beau releasing a pair of RP from its wing rails against a jungle target, 1945. The profuse cordite fumes from initial ignition of the rocket motors were no hazard to the aircraft, but could be unpleasant to the crew inside./*via D Vincent*

Bottom right: A remarkable photo of a pair of 3-inch rocket projectiles at a fraction of a second after being fired from their wing rails. Aircraft is Beau '2-V' of 404 Squadron RCAF, and the RP heads are 60lb HE (High Explosive). /*Imperial War Museum*

Top left: Sliding the last RP onto its guide rail; another quartet of 25lb SAP headed projectiles.

Centre left: WAITING FOR THE 'OFF'. Beau X's of 236 Squadron in October 1944, loaded and ready for another anti-shipping strike. MB-X was NE432.

Below: FINAL TOUCH. Sergeant Herb Cossaboom, RCAF plugging in RP 'pigtails' to their individual aircraft electrical sockets in the main wing. The final safety measure was to plug in the armament safety-break plug, usually situated in the port wing stub. Beau TFX of 404 Squadron RCAF, Davidstow Moor, Cornwall, August 21st, 1944. /*Publich Archives of Canada*

Right: AT THE RECEIVING END. Operating from Berka 3 airfield (near Benghazi, Libya), a Beau of 16 Squadron SAAF recorded this attack on a yacht at Kithera on April 15th, 1944, from a height between 20 and 100 ft.

Below right: OVER-KILL. Dramatic view of an enemy tanker erupting in flames during a Coastal Command Beau strike in the Skagerrak on Sunday, October 15th, 1944, by aircraft of 404 Squadron RCAF. This tanker, and an escorting flak ship were sunk, with no losses to the Beaus. Left and right of the picture can be seen a full salvo of RP burning towards the already-doomed tanker./*British Official*

Coastal Strikes

NORMAN CARR

I joined 143 Squadron at the beginning of November 1943 at Portreath, Cornwall. The squadron was then flying Mk VIc Beaufighters and engaged on long range fighter patrols in the Bay of Biscay and south-western approaches. My navigator was Arthur Tilley, from Chadwell Heath, whom I had first met on a General Reconnaissance course at Charlottetown a year before, and after going our separate ways, met again at 2(C) OTU, Catfoss. I suppose it was inevitable that we should crew up at that outwardly nonchalant but inwardly rather fearful ritual, where no

doubt every pilot and navigator wondered what he was letting himself in for, and then one or the other makes an approach and says, 'What about us getting together?' or something equally inane. I was singularly fortunate; we spent a long time together both on and off-duty with never a disagreement that amounted to anything, and are still in contact to this day. Our first operation was as one of a patrol of three aircraft off the north Spanish coast. Rumour had it that German aircraft were operating in the area and we were sent down to try and in-

COBBER. NE788, one of 455 Squadron RAAF's Beaus, carrying the national flag on its nose. Fully loaded with cannon, machine guns, it also has two 500lb HE bombs carried under the fuselage, with under-wing carriers for two more bombs.
/Imperial War Museum

tercept. We saw nothing and, apart from taking pictures of the local landscape, the first op went off quietly. We were over the first 'hurdle' of starting to really 'belong' to the squadron.

My main impressions of the time spent on this type of operation are of the long hard slogs of six-hour flights, bad weather, endless sea, and sheer relief when a good landfall was made. But at least pilots learnt to fly, navigators to navigate, and operational hours mounted quickly. In February 1944 the squadron moved to North Coates in Lincolnshire, there to become part of the North Coates Strike Wing, comprising 143, 236 and 254 Squadrons. Their purpose was to operate against enemy shipping off the Dutch coast and Friesian Islands, whose place names – Terschelling, Borkum, Dan Helder etc – became as familiar as a street back home. The method of operation was a sea-level trip to the target area, up to about 3,000 feet and close ranks on sighting, attack in quick succession in the following order – anti-flak aircraft with cannons and machine guns; rockets if carried, or further cannons and mg; finally, torpedoes. The secret of success was in good positioning and accurate timing, so that each attack was followed *immediately* by the next. With practice and experience the time taken in actually attacking was, I suppose, remarkably short, but the concentration of fire in such a brief period must have been quite dreadful at the receiving end.

My first experience of a wing strike took place on February 21st, 1944. I was flying Beau 'J' and we attacked a convoy off the Dutch coast. My own target turned out to be an R-Boat. I remember the coloured flak curling up slowly and then whipping past, the spray and smoke around the target (with a slight feeling of amazement that *I* was causing it), then a brief kaleidoscope of ships, wave tops, smoke, aircraft everywhere, and then streaking towards home at sea level. Settling down again on the homeward run there came a feeling of disbelief, then relief that we were unscathed and 'going home'. There was a peculiar mark on my windscreen at eye level which turned out to be a hit by an incendiary bullet. The next few months passed with trips to the Dutch coast either as a Wing or singly on recce; many uneventful, some abortive due to bad weather conditions, and occasionally a convoy strike, all interspersed with training in air firing, formation flying, night flying and low level bombing, the significance of the latter becoming apparent as the year progressed.

In April 1944 our aircraft began being replaced by Mk X's, and at the end of May we were detached to Manston, Kent, for special operations connected with the imminent invasion of Europe. These turned out to be anti-'E' boat ops in the Channel and took the form of armed patrols in force, usually singly or in pairs in conjunction with flare-dropping

Swordfish, Albacores and Wellingtons, or operating singly under a ground control. Two 500lb and two 250lb HE bombs were carried, which meant of course that entry and exit could only be made through the emergency hatch. It was a matter of conjecture how one got out in a hurry – though from experience I can vouch that it could be done . . . This was a period of great activity – from the days of six-hour patrols, it was now possible to make a couple of trips and attacks in one night and log no more than three hours. My most vivid memory of those days was an operation on September 1st, flying Beau 'Z'. Flying alone on ground control, we were directed onto a target and, diving to attack somewhere between Cap Gris Nez and Boulogne, the sea and sky suddenly burst forth with a firework display of no mean proportions and I belatedly realised I was over the middle of a large convoy, with every ship giving me its personal and undivided attention. At a guess I should think it was the German evacuation of Boulogne. As my bombs released I felt a thump and the aircraft gave every indication of a lost engine by slewing to port and dropping a wing. Fortunately for Arthur and me I resisted the natural temptation of going on one engine immediately, and a quick glance around the instruments showed everything apparently working normally. Full right rudder and aileron and more power got us slowly to starboard away from the convoy, and from sea level to a more reasonable

Top left: **ROLLING. Beaus of 455 Squadron RAAF begin to stream for take-off, 1944. UB-N is Beau NE207. RP rails are loaded with 25lb SAP headed rockets.**/*RAAF Photo*

Centre left: **PEEL-OFF. Beau X,NT850, MB-T of 236 Squadron shows its belly as it puts on full bank prior to an attack, late 1944.**/*Imperial War Museum*

Bottom left: **MAST HEIGHT. On July 15th, 1944, Coastal Command mounted one of their largest strikes, surprising a German convoy off the south coast of Norway. Nearly every vessel was either sunk or left blazing. In this view an armed trawler has just received 'close attention' by one of the RP/ Cannon Beaus.**/*British Official*

Above: **TOMMY II. Another TFX of 236 Squadron coded MB-T, in this case LZ293. Note completely different paint scheme applied in comparison with previous two photos.** /*Imperial War Museum*

Centre left: **Coastal Command Beaus jinking their way over a German convoy off the Friesian Islands on March 29th, 1944.** /*British Official*

Bottom left: **A second view of NT850, 'T-TOMMY' of 236 Squadron.**/*MOD (Air)*

111

height. We made our skidding, crabbing, indirect way back to Manston and landed wheels up at rather high speed. Neither of us was hurt and the Beau was found to have been hit in the port wing, cutting aileron controls and pushing a petrol tank up through the wing.

These night operations continued until the squadron rejoined the North Coates Wing on September 8th. A considerable number of sweeps and patrols were carried out off the Dutch coast during September and October, but targets were becoming scarcer and it was with little surprise that towards the end of October the squadron moved north to become part of the Banff Strike Wing, operating against shipping along the coast of German-held Norway. Immediately conversion to Mosquitos (Mk VI's) took place and in a very short time 143 Squadron was taking part in operations requiring a rather different technique of attacking targets in the narrow, precipitous, bleak but beautiful fiords of Norway.

Regarding the Beaufighter as a strike aircraft, it was heavy but immensely strong and powerful. First solos in it were quite awesome for young, comparatively inexperienced pilots. The usual procedure was to switch from Blenheims but, of course, there was no such thing as dual control instruction. You stood behind the pilot and tried to absorb the array of dials and controls and whatever was being ex-

plained. Then a practice on a static cockpit until the dreaded words, 'Off you go'. The power seemed unbelievable on first take-off, and the elation of achievement after that first flight and safe landing something to remember always. Beau pilots grew very fond of their aircraft. Provided you used a bit of muscle it was quite capable of being thrown about the sky. It was reliable and capable of taking an awful beating and still get you home in one piece. I have witnessed Beaus crash-land with a most appalling thump and crew climb out none the worse, where lesser aircraft would have been spread out all over the airfield. I am personally of the opinion that everyone who flew Beaus for any length of time would be hard pressed to find real faults in what was an outstanding aircraft of its time.

SHIP PARTY. Probably the most famous Beaufighter action photo of the war, the occasion was an anti-shipping strike by 455 and 489 Squadrons in the Borkum-Heligoland area on August 25th, 1944. In this 'still' a total of 9 Beaus can be seen amongst the cordite trails and sea plumes./*Imperial War Museum*

Right: Shipping was by no means the only target for Coastal's Beaus, as this Junkers 88 found to its cost when intercepted over the notorious Bay of Biscay. */Imperial War Museum*

Below: BEAU MEN. Squadron Ledader D L Cartridge, DFC (holding pet dog) and some of the crews of 248 Squadron, pictured at Portreath airfield. Flt Sgt Smith (extreme rt, back row) was tragically killed in an air collision on return to base after a strike./*G Medcalf*

Far right: TORBEAU. Nose-on view of an 18-inch torpedo slung underneath a Coastal Beau. The lower, rectangular tail silhouette is that of the torpedo's Mono Air Tail./*Crown copyright*

Right: FISH MEN. Torbeau crew pose with their aircraft. The torpedo crutches and retaining sling can be clearly seen here, though the absence of a Mono Air Tail suggests a pose simply for the news media. With a war head affixed a torpedo (or 'Fish', as they were known to all RAF crews) weighed nearly 1700lb./*Imperial War Museum*

Right: **Rear view of a Torbeau, complete with dummy torpedo, testing the Fairey-Youngman bellows-type wing dive brakes – a modification originally intended for Beau night fighters.**/*Aeroplane*

Below: **FISH PORTER. Beau NE221 in one of several operational roles undertaken by this particular aircraft. It originally served as HU-P with 406 Squadron RCAF as a night fighter; and later served as 'V' of 176 Squadron.**/*Central Press*

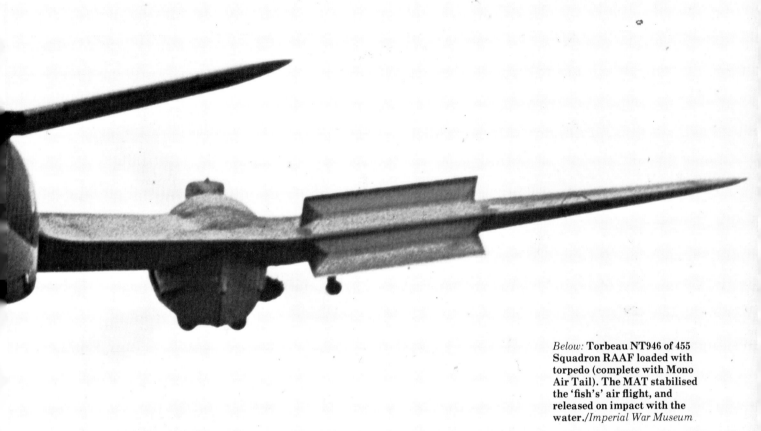

Below: **Torbeau NT946 of 455 Squadron RAAF loaded with torpedo (complete with Mono Air Tail). The MAT stabilised the 'fish's' air flight, and released on impact with the water.**/*Imperial War Museum*

Ship Strike
DUNCAN MARROW

CANNON FURY. EE-C of 404
Squadron RCAF blasting a
German flak-ship in the
Skagerrak, October 15th, 1944.
/Imperial War Museum

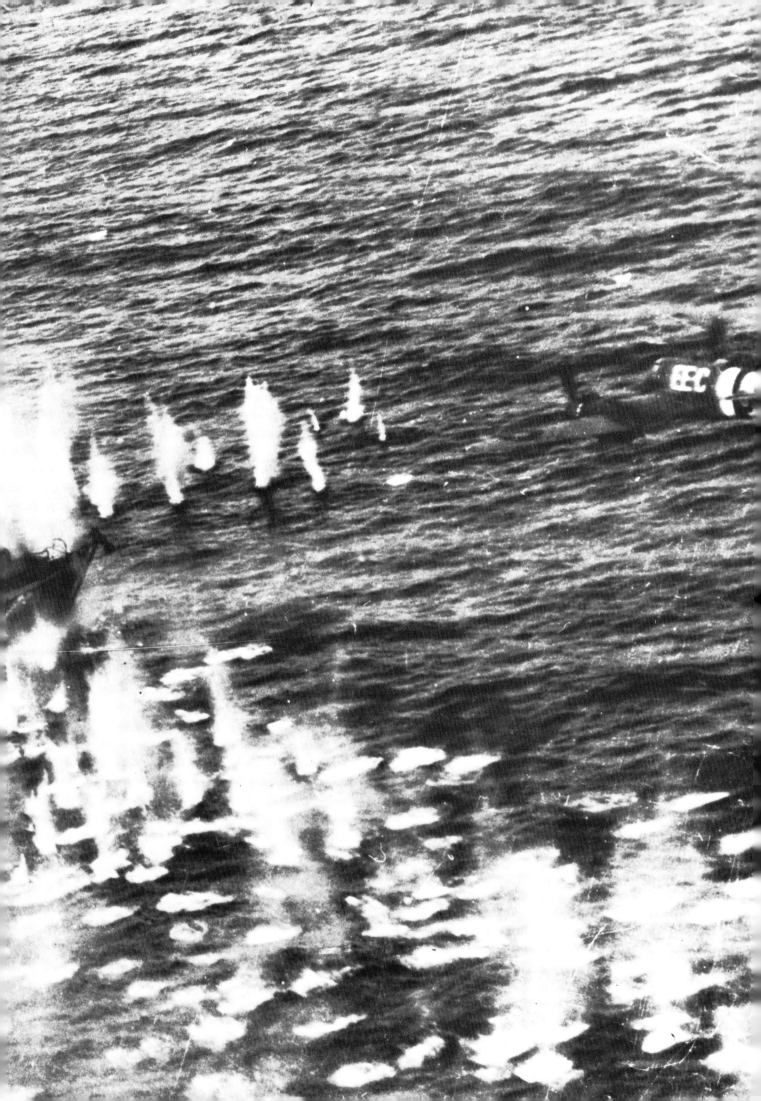

As a navigator, Duncan Marrow completed a total of 102 operational sorties with Coastal Command, the bulk of them in the 'back seat' of a Beaufighter. His first of three operational tours was with 235 and 248 Squadrons '... mainly trying to catch Arado seaplanes in the bay of Biscay – we saw very few, I'm afraid ...', and he then became navigator to Wing Commander Tony Gadd, DFC, the OC Flying at North Coates. His final tour was with another Coastal Beau unit, 144 Squadron. His three years of operational flying earned him a DFC, the Order of Leopold (with palms) and the Belgian *Croix de Guerre*. To tell his full story would need a separate book – the following particular reminiscences merely exemplify the types of sorties undertaken.

'Where to start? At the beginning of course. Catfoss, June 5th 1942 and my first flight in a Beaufighter, just a map-reading and W/T exercise. My pilot, Sgt Norman Smith from Toronto, had done about eight hours in a Beau. After I'd closed down the W/T he said, 'Get on your radio and report an engine failure.' I told him to use his R/T which was not very good, but he did. We went in with a duff engine, and then he did the one thing every pilot is taught not to do – he overshot the runway and went round again. I was told later that we just cleared the hedge at the end of the runway, with black smoke pouring from the bad engine, but we got round and landed safely. Then there was the occasion at Pembry, in south Wales. Smithy and I went on leave when we were at Talbenny, Pembroke,

but as often happened the squadron moved to Pembrey during our absence. We were due back at 0800 hours on November 17th 1942, but Smithy being conscientious returned the previous day (the only conscientious Canadian I've ever heard of ...!) I didn't and travelled overnight. I spent the morning finding all my kit, and intended to find myself a billet in the afternoon. However, the Flight commander had already seen Smithy and put us down to fly on an escort sortie. It was on – off – on – off – and finally we got airborne at 1730 hours, but only just. At about 50 feet up one engine cut, and there was a long hill in front of us. To get round it we had to turn into the dud engine (another thing not to do), then we lost sight of the airfield. Neither of us knew the terrain, and it was the worst possible light, between day and night. We did get round the hill and landed, not bothering with the runway and stopping only feet away from a parked Beaufighter. A sortie on December 30th 1942 added further invaluable experience. We were escorting some naval ships which had picked up a rusty old tanker off the south coast of Ireland. We circled the ships for at least two hours and were then relieved by another Beau. Smithy thought we could fly safely over the ships to have a good look before we left. We did, but every gun in the naval escort followed us – the Navy never did trust us ...

I finished my first tour of 200 hours operational flying in April 1943. The majority of it was spent in the Bay of Biscay, where U-boats were going in and out. We

Above left: **Dallachy Wing, Coastal Command – 144, 455 RAAF and 489 RNZAF Squadrons Beaus at Langham prior to attacks on shipping in Kiel harbour, May 5th, 1945.** */D Marrow, DFC*

Above right: **START-UP. Beau VI's 'B' and 'Q' of 144 Squadron about to start engines.** */D Marrow, DFC*

Centre right: **BEAU TEAM. Wing Commander Tony Gadd, DFC (rt) and his usual navigator, Flt Lt Duncan Marrow, DFC.** */D Marrow, DFC*

Below right: **OVER THE WAVES. NE831, PL-O, 144 Squadron, from Langham, tucks in 'tight and low' during the trans-North Sea leg to Norway for an anti-shipping strike, late 1944.** */D Marrow, DFC*

were mainly after the Arados chasing our Whitleys, but rarely found one. My second tour was with Wing Commander Tony Gadd, who had just returned from Australia where he had been running a torpedo training school. Before the war he had done a great deal of torpedo dropping, mainly in 'Stringbags' (Swordfish), and in fact had dropped probably more torps than any other man, in practice, of course. Our first operational posting was to North Coates, where Tony became Wing Commander Flying i.e he was the station commander's deputy in all things concerned directly with flying. Unlike most Wingcos Flying, at North Coates he actually flew. This being so, he had to have a navigator, which was me, but we weren't on any particular squadron. There were three Beau squadrons there – 143 and 236 armed with cannons and rockets, and 254 with torpedoes. The method of attack had been developed over the years. The whole force formed up over the aerodrome and set course in formation. This meant that the leading navigator was responsible for a good landfall. The other navs did their best to keep their navigational plot going. We found it advantageous to set course using the met man's wind forecast and hold this course for 30 minutes. During that time the direction and speed of the wind had been calculated and a fresh course could be set. This procedure was repeated every half-hour. Our height on setting course was usually 2,000 feet, gradually reducing as we approached the enemy coast to about 10 feet. On sighting a target, up to 2,000 feet again, ready for the attack, but not the torpedo Beaus. The first wave to go in would be the cannon-firing Beaus, which allowed for a certain amount of manoeuvrability. The rocket aircraft followed in a steady dive, and after releasing their rockets they then opened up with cannons. The torpedoes had to be dropped when the aircraft was flying perfectly level at 100 feet and at 180 knots speed. Naturally, they would have been sitting ducks for the flak, but the function of the cannon and rocket attack was to make the ships' gunners run for cover and thereby give the torpedo boys a clear run in.

We went out once or twice on our own with a torpedo at night, and made a few attacks, but with no success. Then came our *piece de resistance* – June 15th, 1944, just after D-Day. The Air Ministry (or somesuch) had a report that two most important ships were in Dan Helder preparing to sail, with 17 escort vessels of various types. We knew that they were going north, presumably to finish fitting out as they were both on a maiden voyage. Intelligence worked out that though all the ships were capable of 17 knots, they would be mine-sweeping and so their speed would be cut to 12 knots. At that speed they would not reach safe anchorage during the short night. All available Beaufighters of North Coates and Langham Wings were assembled at Langham, totalling 44 aircraft, of which, I think, nine were torpedo Beaus of 254 Squadron led by Wg Cdr Paddy Burns. We had nine Mustangs as fighter cover. Tony Gadd was chosen to lead the whole force, which made me the lead navigator. We took off at 0410 hours and set course. When we reached the target area we found a thin layer of cloud at around 1,000 feet. Tony Gadd and I had a conflab and decided to go above it. The cloud thickened as we went north but, luckily, didn't reach 10/10ths state. Through a break in the cloud we spotted the convoy, sailing serenely on with balloons flying. Tony manoeuvred for position but we were just a little too near the convoy. It takes a hell of a lot of sky to bring 40-odd aircraft through 90 degrees. The formation on the right, which was the inner part of the 'wheel', could not throttle back sufficiently to keep in formation. So the leader took his whole force beneath our force and Tony slipped the middle force to take his place on the right. By that strategy all the Beaus were more or less in line abreast, with the exception of the torpedo boys.

Paddy Burns had gone straight through the cloud to sea level or thereabouts. The convoy spotted his force and started firing

at them. (I remember Paddy saying that his R/T had packed up so that he did not know what was going on above cloud). He got quite close to the ships, almost within dropping range of the torpedoes, then wham – through the clouds came about three dozen aircraft with guns a-blazing. The ships were swamped with cannon shells and rockets, and Paddy and his boys had a clear run in. I believe that two torpedoes went into one ship, and three in the other. From my log, I see two merchant vessels and one escort were sunk, six seriously damaged, four damaged and one escort left calling for assistance. And a recce afterwards reported that the balloons were still flying from the sunken ships. All our Beaus returned. I've always regarded this strike as a triumph of co-operation. Four factors made the success possible: (a) the people who first gave the information, (b) the Intelligence bods who worked it out perfectly, (c) the weather man who sent the cloud to exactly the right spot, and (d) the formation leaders who so expertly changed places without a word. For this episode Tony Gadd was awarded a DFC, and Paddy Burns got a bar to his DFC.

Next day, June 16th, Tony and I flew down to Northolt where we were whisked off to Broadcasting House in London to give an account of the strike to the nation in 'War Report' after the nine o'clock news. We spent the afternoon with a member of the BBC staff, getting the story condensed into 2½ minutes (all we were allowed). Then we bogged off for a meal and a visit to a news theatre, arriving back at the studio about 9 pm. There John Snagge was just rehearsing what he

had to say about Tony . . . 'has dropped over 1100 torpedoes *in action*'. Tony soon put him right – he would never have lived it down!

There were occasional 'hairy' moments, such as the time I was flying in Beau NE770 and one of our blokes' rockets went through our port wing, It went straight through the main spar, which was sheet metal with strengthening at top and bottom. It just started to cut through the bottom. (A couple of inches lower and I wouldn't be telling this story . . .) Then it went through the petrol tank and out, leaving a fin behind which I still have. A less serious occasion was whilst we were at Banff and six aircraft went down to Bircham Newton. I was doing the lead navigation – or was supposed to have been. The weather was bad and I, being a lazy type, just plotted a series of *GEE* fixes which would keep us clear of Flamborough Head. I saw the Head (as I thought) and was happy. Then all hell broke loose up front as the real Flamborough Head loomed up – the other was Filey Head, and my 'navigation' was taking us slap into the cliffs – I was *not* very popular. Another amusing effort was when we were on detachment to Davidstow Moor in Cornwall. At the time the Germans were pinned in the Brest peninsula and we were sinking any ships which might be evacuating them. We went down the coast of France map-reading. I said, 'Outside Ile de Groix' which was close to the shore opposite Lorient and, of course, well defended. 'Inside Ile de Yeu and Belle Ile'. We attacked some ships in Les Sable d'Olonne and as usual got split up. Some

Three progressive views of 144 Squadron's Beaus strafing a German merchant vessel which was anchored close to a mountain wall in a Norwegian fiord./*R Field*

of the blokes, recognising our Beau, formated on us for the return. We passed inside Belle Ile and Ile de Yeu, when I said I'd make a report to base, turned to the radio and didn't look up for about 10 minutes, being busy making out the message and transmitting it. When I did look up there was land on the *port* side, where there should have been sea. Tony thought we had come this way, inside Ile de Groix. It being too late to turn back, we had to go through. Only one pilot followed us, the others went round the island and climbed up to see the fun. Jerry chucked all he could lay his hands on at us from both sides, but Tony and the other pilot (who said he enjoyed it . . .) jigged up and down, and only one small bullet found its mark. Tony could see the heavy stuff dropping into the water in front of the nose, and I could see tracers coming for us and turning away at the last minute.

Below: **SPOT-ON.** Rocket-firing Beaus register bulls-eyes on an armed trawler off the Dutch coast, 1944. A second salvo of RP can be seen on their way to the target./*British Official*

Left: **MIXING IT.** Australian crews of 455 Squadron RAAF contributing their share to the two-Wing Coastal Command mass strike against enemy shipping off Mandal, Norwegian coast, on July 15th, 1944./*Australian War Memorial*

Right: **GOING HOME.** Beaus of 143 Squadron returning to Portreath, 1943, after a patrol. /*N Carr*

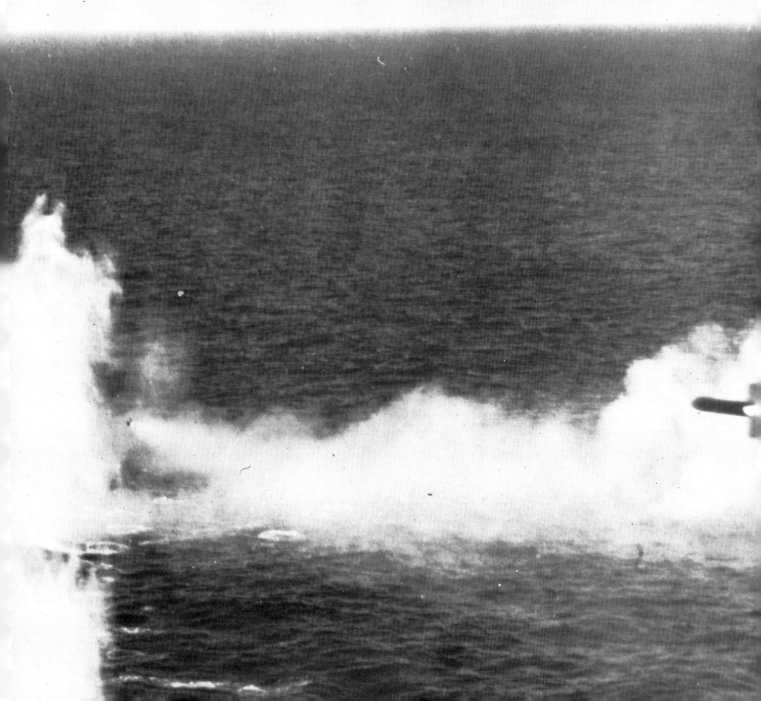

Coastal Canucks

No.404 ('Buffalo') Squadron, RCAF was the second squadron to be formed overseas by the RCAF in World War 2, and the first Canadian unit in Coastal Command. In the event it remained the RCAF's only Coastal fighter unit throughout the war. Formed at Thorney Island, Hampshire on April 15th 1941, the squadron moved base several times during the following months before arriving at Dyce, Scotland in October 1941 and commenced a distinguished operational career flying Blenheim IVs. By December the squadron was wholly based at Sum-

burgh (the 'Awful Place' as the squadron diary records the move...) and on December 18th first 'drew blood' when the squadron commander, Wing Commander P. H. Woodruff, DFC, and his crew intercepted a Ju 88 weather aircraft some 50 miles east of Sumburgh and shot it down. During the following nine months the 'Buffaloes' carried out intensive operations, mainly in the form of anti-shipping patrols and general escort cover for other aircraft across the North Sea and along the Norwegian coast. These sorties often involved combat with

Beau '2-G' of 404 Squadron RCAF, being loaded with RP, revs-up for taxying as the armourers plug in the RP 'pigtail' electrical leads.
/Imperial War Museum

the Luftwaffe and despite their aging aircraft 404's crews gave a good account of themselves, claiming several victories. In September 1942 the 'Buffaloes' returned (somewhat reluctantly. . .) to the dubious delights of Dyce aerodrome, where they finally exchanged their outdated Blenheims for Beaufighters, 15 Beaus being received by the end of the month. In the following month command of 404 passed into the very capable hands of Wing Commander G. G. Truscott, a former test pilot. At the end of January 1943 the squadron moved south to Chivenor, Devon, there to participate in Coastal Command's constant battle in the Bay of Biscay by providing top cover for the Command's far-ranging anti-submarine aircraft. By April 1943, however, the 'Buffaloes' were once more in Scotland, based now at Wick and soon involved in hotly-fought actions against German convoys and their deadly escort flak ships off the Norwegian coast.

The first such sortie was flown on April 27th, when 404 provided top cover and 'neutralising' action against a convoy

being attacked by torpedo-carrying Beaus of its sister unit, 144 Squadron. 404's Beaus swept ahead of the torpedo Beaus, smothering the flak ships with a 'blanket' of cannon and machine gun fire, leaving 144's aircraft to make their torpedo runs virtually unmolested. One vessel was hit by three torpedoes, while two Beaus were damaged by flak. One of these, piloted by Fg Off Schoales, received serious damage and Schoales, wounded in the left arm, earned a DFC for bringing his Beau back to base safely (the second time he had brought home a damaged aircraft from Norway). Luftwaffe opposition to these sorties became increasingly stiffer, as on May 14th when Flt Lt J. T. McCutcheon spotted a Blohm and Voss flying boat and promptly attacked. During the fight the Beau was hit several times by flak, setting the port engine on fire and damaging the undercarriage. McCutcheon pressed home his attack and raked the flying boat with cannon fire, until with two of its

three engines ablaze, the flying boat hit the sea. Despite the condition of his Beau, McCutcheon next tackled a pair of Focke Wulf 190s – which immediately fled! Extinguishing the engine fire, the pilot set course for home and nursed the crippled Beau across the North Sea to finally make a skilful belly landing at base. This, and other feats, brought McCutcheon a DFC award in July.

July 28th, 1943 proved to be a 'star' day for 404's crews. In the morning two Beaus, piloted by Sqn Ldr A. L. de La Haye and Fg Off Sid Shulemson (his first operational sortie), took off to act as air cover for a naval formation. A BV 138 flying boat was soon spotted and De la Haye made a head-on attack, splashing cannon strikes on the German's engines and wings. Sid Shulemson followed in with a stern attack and the flying boat burst into flames and pancaked onto the sea. Sighting a second BV138, De la Haye attacked from its stern, firing from 400 to 200 yards, and the flying boat dove straight into the sea in flames. Later the same day Fg Off E. J. Keefe sighted another pair of BV 138's and attacked. His fire damaged the first, while the second was hit in its port engine and hull and burst into flames. It was learned later that this flying boat had to ditch in the sea, the surviving crew being picked up by a German U-boat. This U-boat was sunk a few days later, and among the survivors were the crew of Keefe's victim!

In August 404's Beaus were sent to Leuchars for fitting with rocket projectile (RP) equipment, while the crews were detached to Tain for RP training. By the following month the squadron was operational again, as part of a newly-formed Strike Wing. The period of training at Tain was not without incident. Flt Lt Len Barcham, DFC, an Englishman posted to the unit, recalled, 'I personally can vouch for the strength of a Beau. Whilst detached at Tain for the month of August 1943 we were doing lots of circuits and bumps, trying to find the best and most accurate way to fire the RP (with concrete practice heads) in 'singles', 'pairs' and 'salvoes' at a nearby target. No navigation being necessary, we had agreed on the 29th to give a ground erk a flip (his first ever), and he was sitting in the navigator's seat under the rear cupola; whilst I was standing astride the well behind the pilot, Fg Off Johnny Symons, calling out and checking various angles of attack, speeds etc while he concentrated on the target. One engine then lost all its oil, seized up solid and wouldn't feather, and we went more or

128

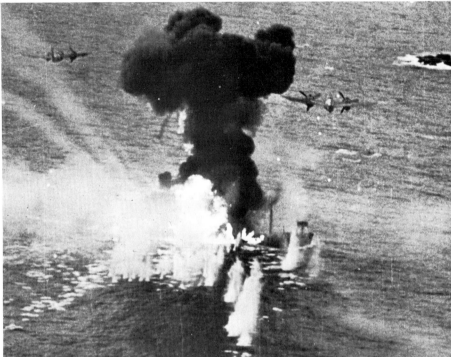

less where the Beau took us downwards towards Clashmore Wood, north of Tain. We finished up in a clearing in the woods where the trees had been cut down to about two feet high stumps, and these literally tore the Beau to bits each time we bounced. With the rockets and cannons firing *of their own accord*, it was something of a panic, and when we eventually settled, we had about the front 10 feet of the aircraft left! Though bruised, we got out rather smartly – our poor passenger had been shot out about two bumps previously and we watched him disappearing at a great rate of knots over a nearby hill. (Frankly, I've never seen him since...) Whilst we were still virtually in the circuit, we were now north of Dornoch Firth, and nobody had the faintest idea where we were. We set forth on foot to find some way of getting a message back to base and eventually at a farm were offered two bikes. I must have thought I'd had enough for one day – because I remember I refused to ride mine since it had no brakes and it was all down-hill to the nearest village and 'phone. We were eventually picked up by transport – a journey of about 25 miles inland and round by Bonai Bridge to get back to Tain.'

During November and December 1943 the anti-shipping offensive was stepped up considerably. On December 16th four Beaus from 404 took off for an anti-convoy strike, but just after lifting off the runway Beau 'G-George' (Fg Off J.S. Cummins and Warrant Officer K McGrath) had its starboard engine fail

completely. An immediate attempt to land on the remaining motor failed and the Beau crashed and began to burn. Cummins, the pilot, was unconscious and trapped in his cockpit by the control column pressing into his stomach and his right foot locked under a smashed rudder bar. McGrath managed to free himself and went forward to extricate his pilot by removing the safety harness and his right boot, despite the fact that at any second the fuel tanks and ammunition load could explode. Suffering from burns to his face and hands, McGrath dragged Cummin's inert body 100 yards away from the burning Beaufighter to a nearby farmhouse. A few seconds later the squadron medical officer, Flt Lt G. C. Beacock arrived at the crash and, unaware that the crew were already safe, plunged into the flaming wreckage attempting to rescue them. For their selfless courage McGrath was awarded a George Medal and Beacock a Mention in Despatches.

The shipping strikes continued in February and March 1944, and culminated in a combined strike against the 14,000 ton troopship *Monte Rosa* on March 30th. Nine Beaus from 404 with nine more from 144 Squadron, all led by 404's commander, Wg Cdr C. A. Willis, DFC. They found their target just off Haugesund, well protected by escort vessels and a large number of Luftwaffe fighters. Willis deployed his formation and then led them in through a veritable wall of flak. The troopship was finally left smoking and burning, whilst Fg Off J. Rancourt in Beau 'K' completed his

Top left: **BUFFALO BEAU. NE355, EE-H of 404 Squadron RCAF at Davidstow, Moor, Cornwall, August 21st, 1944. The 'tube' protruding from the nose was a Fairchild nose camera mounting.**/*Public Archives of Canada*

Centre left: **TEAMWORK. A pair of 404 Squadron's Beaus, working in concert, destroy a tanker in the Skagerrak on October 15th, 1944.**

Bottom left: **'FOR WHAT WE ARE ABOUT TO RECEIVE ...' German flak ship, already burning from a previous onslaught, about to be hit by another salvo of rockets. Bourgeneuf, French coast, August 8th, 1944.**/*L Barcham, DFC*

Below: **CAULDRON. The German 'Sperrbrecher' (merchant vessel) MAGDEBURG engulfed in cannon RP strikes off Royan on August 13th, 1944 – a combined 236 and 404 Squadrons' strike. It sank the same day.** /*D Marrow, DFC*

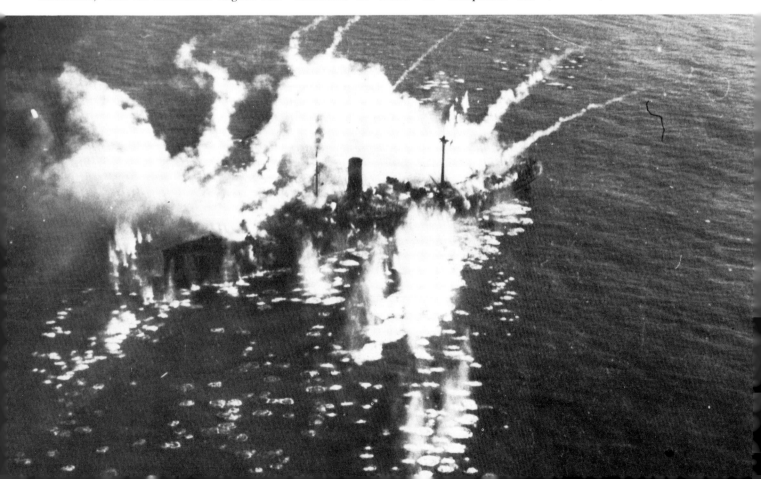

attack by attacking three Me 109s and shooting one down in flames. Two Beau crews were lost, one of them Wg Cdr Willis, though it was later learned that he was a prisoner of war. Command of 404 now passed to a Flight commander, Wing Commander Ken Gatward, DFC, an Englishman who made Beaufighter history on June 12th, 1942 when he flew a lone sortie over Paris and dropped two French tricolours near the Arc de Triomphe and rounded out his sortie by blasting the local Gestapo headquarters with his cannons. Shortly after his appointment, 404 moved south yet again, this time to Davidstow Moor in Cornwall in preparation for the imminent Allied invasion of Europe.

On June 6th (D-Day) 404 was part of a three-squadron strike (with 144 and 235 Squadrons) against three German destroyers attempting to hit the flanks of the Allied invasion fleet crossing the English Channel. With Sid Shulemson leading the 'Buffalo' contingent, the Beaus came out of the sun and achieved complete surprise. Both the leading and centre destroyers were pounded with rockets and cannons, and both were left burning furiously when the strike force

finally withdrew. The rear destroyer had drawn alongside the centre vessel for protection, but Fg Off J. D. Taylor swung out of the formation, skirted round the 'protecting' vessel and poured a salvo of RP and 500 rounds of cannonfire into the 'reluctant' vessel. Early next morning the Beaus returned and hit the destroyers again, setting one ablaze; whilst the Royal Navy forced one destroyer aground where it was shot to pieces by 404 Squadron in an RP attack on June 9th. As the Allied invasion forces gained a firm foothold in Normandy, the 'Buffaloes' were moved back north (the 13th move of base since the unit's original formation . . .) and were temporarily based at Strubby on the Lincolnshire coast. Anti-shipping strikes in the Heligoland Bight and the coastal waters of the Netherlands were continued; though a detachment of the squadron was hastily recalled in August to assist in strikes against German naval forces in the Bay of Biscay. On August 7th Ken Gatward landed his Beau at Cherbourg, his being the first aircraft of Coastal Command to land on European soil since D-Day.

Gatward's 'swan song' with the 'Buffaloes' came on August 21st when he

Above: **404 Squadron personnel who participated in the D-Day (June 6th, 1944) attack which destroyed one and damaged two German destroyers. L-R: Fg Offs Roger Savard; P R Bassett; S S ('Slippery Sid') Shulemson; P A 'Pappy' Powell; Flt Lt A H Hodson; 'Uncle Herman' mascot; Lt S B Rossiter, USAF; Flt Lt C H 'Chuck' Taylor; and Fg Off R A Wallace. Davidstow Moor, June 10th, 1944.**/*Public Archives of Canada*

Left: **BEGINNER'S LUCK. Blohm und Voss BV 138 flying boat shot down off Scotland on August 28th, 1943 by Sqn Ldr De la Haye and Fg Off Sid Shulemson – it was Shulemson's *first* operational sortie! (See text).**/*Public Archives of Canada*

led a particularly successful strike, and was then awarded a DSO and posted as a liaison officer to Paris (appropriately). He was succeeded in command of 404 by Wing Commander E. W. Pierce who remained CO until the end of hostilities in 1945. With the new commander came another move of base when the squadron were sent to Banff early in September. On September 14th an eventful strike was made against six enemy vessels off Kristiansund. The flak opposition was fierce. Fg Off M. Baribeau was forced to ditch (with his navigator, Flt Lt C. H. Taylor, killed) and was picked up by the Germans; Sqn Ldr Schoale, DFC had to nurse a crippled Beau back to base – again; whilst a third crew, Fg Offs A. Menaul and J. Tomes, won immediate DFCs for their part in the attack. An exploding shell shattered the pilot's windscreen, wounding Menaul in the arm, shoulder, chest and face, yet he completed his attack. Tomes then came forward and, after helping Menaul regain full control, administered first aid. Barely able to see through the shattered windscreen, Menaul nevertheless accomplished a safe landing back at Banff. From Banff the squadron moved westward to Dallachy – the fourth unit move since May – and continued their anti-shipping offensive. Six vessels were sunk or seriously damaged during two November strikes alone; and on December 9th the 'Buffaloes' destroyed another which was hit by at least 30 rockets and erupted in two violent explosions before being beached. In this attack Fg Off A. K. Cooper and WO C. F. Smith, on only their second operational sortie with 404, carried their attack so close that their Beau struck the vessel's mast. The impact tore away the Beau's wing and it hit the sea and exploded.

1945 opened with a week of concentrated action when, in 11 days, the 'Buffaloes' took part in five strikes against enemy shipping; on one occasion against a ship sheltering at the foot of some high, steep cliffs. Some of the Beaus made three runs against this target, coming in so close that they were struck by rock fragments and other flying debris. By then the Germans were pulling their naval and military forces out of Norway in a desperate last fling to protect the crumbling Reich at home, and on February 9th the 'Buffaloes' were sent to attack a flotilla of 11 ships sheltering in a fiord before it could sail. Strongly defended by shore flak batteries, its own defensive guns and a Luftwaffe fighter cover of a dozen Fw 190s, the flotilla was a

formidable target. A total of 46 Beaus were despatched to attack, with Sqn Ldr Christison leading 404's eleven Beaus. Roaring down the narrow fiord, the 'Buffaloes' hit at least four ships, shot down one aircraft and damaged a second (both of these by Fg Off J. E. Nelson who was later awarded a DFC). But the curtain of murderous flak took a tragic toll. Six of 404's Beaus were shot down, with only one (Fg Off Roger Savard) of the 12 crew members surviving. It was the squadron's 'Black Friday' – the most severe loss by the squadron in its long career. Three shipping strikes in March 1945 brought further losses. On March 8th Fg Off R. C. Ridge and his navigator, Plt Off P. McCartney were hit by flak and crashed. This crew had almost completed their tour of operations, having joined the squadron exactly one year before. March 24th brought the loss of two more crews. Sqn Ldr Christison, by then the oldest member of the squadron, led a 44-aircraft strike near Egersund Harbour against a force of six vessels. Diving through the

Above: **'WHAT DID THAT ? MICE! . . . Fg Off Herby Hallett points to flak damage in the port wing of his 404 Squadron Beau TFX, Davidstow Moor, August 21st, 1944./***Public Archives of Canada***

Top right: **DE-BRIEFED. Crews of 404 Squadron after a sortie on August 21st, 1944, Davidstow Moor, Cornwall. Identified, from left: Unknown; 'Red' McGrath; French; Unknown; Herby Hallet; Wg Cdr Ken Gatward, DSO, DFC (wiping face); Ivor Johnsson. /***Public Archives of Canada***

Centre right: **TEA AND WADS. Air and ground crews of 404 Squadron taking a welcome break with refreshments from the Church of Scotland's mobile canteen. RAF Tain, Scotland, July 29th, 1943. In background is Beau *'MORNING GLORY'*, the mount of Fg Off Ivor Johnsson./***Public Archives of Canada***

dense flak, Christison's aircraft was hit by a shell in the starboard engine. Moments later Christison's voice was heard over the R/T to say his navigator, Flt Lt Freddy Toone, DFC was wounded, and that the Beau was so badly damaged that he was going to have to ditch. He was seen to go down about 10 miles off the Norwegian coast. The second loss was the Beau flown by Flt Ltd L. R. Aljoe and Flt Sgt C. E. Orser, which was also a victim of flak and ditched near the coast. These were, in fact, the squadron's last war casualties. It was also the last operation by the 'Buffaloes' with Beaufighters because they were then re-equipped with Mosquitos at Banff early in April.

On April 22nd the Canadians returned to operations in their new aircraft with a vengeance, when Fg Off D. A. Catrano strafed a BV 138 flying boat and a Heinkel 115 anchored just off-shore and left the flying boat blazing. The unit's last war mission came on May 4th when Wg Cdr Pierce led his Mossies and 55 other aircraft on a shipping strike near Kiel,

attacking at such close range that one Mosquito returned with part of the mast and the ensign of the German destroyer attached to it. They left behind them seven, possibly eight badly damaged ships. On May 25th, 1945 four years after its formation, 404 Squadron was officially disbanded. Its war tally was prodigious. Approximately 215 enemy ships were attacked, with a tonnage of 30,363 sunk and 23,272 damaged. In addition 28 enemy aircraft had been destroyed, and four U-boats either sunk or at least severely damaged. The cost in personnel and aircraft had not been small, however. 113 crew members had been killed or reported 'missing' and three others were known to be prisoners of war. In recognition of individual courage a total of 70 gallantry awards were made up to the date of disbandment. The squadron's official badge, officially approved in March 1943, carries a buffalo head as its central motif; whilst its motto, 'Ready to Fight' could hardly have been more appropriate.

Beaus were Tough

Below: **A8-89 of 22 Squadron RAAF after a forced landing at Tarakan on June 29th, 1945.**
/G Pentland

Right: **BITS AND PIECES. A8-129 (SK-K) of 93 Squadron RAAF which stalled during landing at Labuan strip on August 16th, 1945, and crashed 300 yards south-east of the runway. The crew, Ellers and Dunn, though badly injured and shocked, survived.**
/E W Robinson

Top left: **SPREADING IT AROUND.** Beau VIF, X8216 (KP-M) of 409 Squadron RCAF scattered around a field adjacent to RAF Acklington.
/J P Small

Below left: **THE AMERICAN WAY.** Two views of a 416th Squadron USAF Beaufighter which 'fell out of the sky' at RAF Acklington.
/J P Small

Top right: Beau VI, EL439 of 27 Squadron (WO Ron Thorogood and Fg Off Edgar Welch) which landed at Agartala, Burma with defective brakes on July 4th, 1943; hit the Air Traffic tower; and fell into basic assembly components. The crew just walked away . . .
/Sqn Ldr E S Welch

Centre right: **BELLY-FLOP.** NE775 of 455 Squadron RAAF after an hydraulics failure during landing, 1944. Note inflated dinghy on wing.
/F Smith

Below right: **COMBAT VICTIM.** A Coastal Command Beau, JL725, piloted by Fg Off H J Thomas, was forced to do a wheels-up landing after a fierce combat with a pair of Messerschmitt Bf 109s. Note wing machine gun ports. In background (under starboard wing) is a Handley Page 'Sparrow' (transport version of the pre-war Harrow bomber).
/Imperial War Museum

Left: **TAIL TROUBLE** – the aftermath of a low-level train-busting sortie./*Imperial War Museum*

Below left: **STRAFING HAZARD.** This Beau of a desert squadron hit a telegraph pole at full speed during a strafe of lorry convoys on the Libyan coast. It flew 400 miles back to base and landed safely. /*Imperial War Museum*

Right: **TALE OF A TAIL.** Sergeant James, a desert Beau pilot, suffered this damage as he fought two enemy aircraft – but he came back./*Imperial War Museum*

Below right: **SOUVENIR.** Fg Off Lee Turner, navigator (left) and Fg Off Steve Sykes, an Australian crew of 455 Sqn RAAF examining the 'souvenirs' they brought back from a convoy attack in the Den Helder anchorage on September 12th, 1944. The souvenir is the 3-feet top of an armed trawler's mast, which was embedded in their Beau's nose. Sykes was awarded a DFC for this sortie; while in May 1945 he was also awarded a DSO for an attack on a ship in Ardals Fiord, Norway when, despite severe arm and leg flak injuries, he continued his attack; then flew 350 miles back to base and landed safely. /*British Official*

Aussie Beaus

When in early 1942 the Japanese swept all Allied opposition aside and finally occupied Malaya, Burma, Sumatra, Borneo and myriad surrounding islands across the Pacific Ocean, Australia was left virtually defenceless. Bereft of the traditional Royal Navy first-line protection the continent was faced with an imminent invasion by the Japanese – and had little with which to thwart such an attack. Aggravating her problem was the fact that a large proportion of her trained and experienced Servicemen were serving with the Allied forces in Europe and the Middle East operational theatres, and these could not be retrieved without seriously depleting the near-desperate state of the Allies already fighting in those areas. Supported to a degree by elements of the USAAF, the Australians prepared to defend their homeland with their own resources. Existing equipment for the struggle to come was poor and scarce, obsolete in many cases and far too little in overall quantity. In particular the RAAF needed modern aircraft, capable of long range bombing and capable of anti-shipping strikes. Just before the war the Australian government had chosen the Bristol Beaufort for local manufacture, and on July 1st, 1939 a total of 90

Beauforts for the RAAF was contracted. At the same time planning for future RAAF establishments recommended that the Beaufighter would become a standard long range fighter for the Service.

The outbreak of war and subsequent delays in policy held up final decisions on the future use of the Beau, but on May 20th, 1941, the War Cabinet authorised the purchase of 54 Beaufighters from the UK; 12 machines to be delivered by December of that year, and the remainder by March 1942. It also recommended that parallel Beaufort/Beaufighter production be undertaken in Australia – the decision again being delayed, this time due to the new possibility that manufacture of the DH Mosquito could be carried out in Australia, and this aircraft could replace the Beaufighter in its required role. In April 1942 permission was granted for Australia to retain the first 90 Beaufighters to be built locally, but in the same month, on April 20th, the first UK Beau arrived in Australia. By May 8th a total of 54 Beaus ex-UK had been received or were in transit ships en route. These and all subsequent Beaufighters received from Britain were re-serialled as A19- series, a total of 217 Beaus being involved.

The first RAAF unit to equip with Beaufighters was 30 Squadron, RAAF, which formed officially on March 9th, 1942, and flew its first battle sorties on September 17th of that year – strafing Japanese positions along Buna beach. A second squadron, No 31, was formed on August 14th, 1942, and flew its first operational sorties on November 17th. Meanwhile the question of producing 'home-grown' Beaufighters had been finally agreed and in January 1943 Australian production started at Fisherman's Bend factories under the auspices of the Department of Aircraft Production (DAP). Of the 450 total originally ordered, 364 were eventually

HYBRID. Typical Aussie 'know-how' illustrated by the melding of a tail section from A19-205 (LY-P) and the main fuselage of LY-M. 30 Squadron RAAF, Bougainville./*RAAF Official*

built and delivered to the RAAF, all serialled in the A8- series. The first production Beau, A8-1, made its first flight on May 26th, 1944 and five days later deliveries to the RAAF commenced.

Only three more operational units were equipped with Beaus, Nos 22, 92 and 93 Squadrons. 22 Squadron, a veteran unit flying Douglas Bostons, began exchanging (reluctantly, it should be said) their faithful Bostons for Beaus in December 1944, and became fully operational again on February 9th, 1945; whilst the last to be Beau-equipped, 93 Squadron, was formed on January 22nd, 1945 and only managed to fly two operations before the Japanese surrender and the end of the war.

The full story of the Australian Beaufighters and their crews, though well detailed generally in the excellent four-volume Australian official history of the air war, demands a separate book to do ample justice. More particularly so because very few accurate accounts of them have appeared outside Australia. Indeed, the magnificent and arduous three years war fought by the Australians against the Japanese is largely ignored or simply unknown by a majority of military historians, if one is to judge by published material over the past 30 years. Flying and fighting over jungle and ocean, in primitive conditions of accommodation, maintenance, supply; and in climatic conditions described as 'the worst in the world', the Australian Beau crews, air and ground, are long overdue for recognition. As their weapon of war, the Beaufighter was liked and respected by its crews. It proved nearly ideal for the (mainly) low level form of operations on which it was employed; was tough and pugnacious, reliable and faithful. Even in the rarer role of pure air fighting, the Beau upheld its international reputation.

Top left: A19-120, LY-H of 30 Squadron RAAF taking off from Bougainville./F Smith

Centre left: Beau TFX A8-1, the first Australian-built example, which first flew on May 26th, 1944. It served at No. 1 APU later. The 'blister' mounting on the nose was a fairing for a Sperry auto-pilot, though this item was rarely installed on operations.

Bottom left: SANGA SANGA SCENE. Panorama of 22 Squadron RAAF's Beaus at dispersal on Sanga Sanga airstrip, in the Phillipines, 1944. DU-H is A8-50.

Top right: EN ROUTE. A8-145, LY-A of 30 Squadron RAAF, piloted by Fg Off Bill Madigan, flying over the Halmaheras on a strike against Hoerokoe, Kairatoe and Namlea enemy-held airstrips, April 1st, 1945. /W Madigan

Centre right: INSIGNIA. Most operational RAAF Beaus in 1945 were individually embellished with cartoon characters and/or particular names by their crews. 93 Squadron ('The Green Ghosts') particularly indulged whims of the crews, as exemplified here by the ghoulish cartoon on the rudder of A8-122. Its crew here are Flt Lt W Harris (pilot) and navigator Ross Shute./R Shute

Right: Another 93 Sqn machine, A8-124, its crew and decoration. Received on the squadron on the squadron on February 2nd, 1945, its usual crew was Flt Sgt N Duckmanton and WO R G Morton, seen here./R Shute

Top right: LONG RANGE. A 22 Squadron RAAF Beau with 180-200 gallon drop tank attached for long range strikes across the Pacific./*E Bulfin*

Centre right: A19-87, 'R' of 30 Squadron RAAF, and ex-RAF Beau originally serialled T5264, over Gasmata, New Britain on July 25th 1943 en route to a jungle target. Pilot was Flt Lt Ted Marron, DFC./*E Marron, DFC*

Below: DUSK PATROL. LY-F of 30 Squadron RAAF prowling along the New Guinea coastline, early 1943, seeking Japanese water transports and barges – a primary task for the unit at that period./*via G Pentland*

Bottom: A8-14 which served with 31 Squadron RAAF, but crashed on March 3rd 1945. /*H Shelton*

Above: **DEPOT SERVICING.**
As in any air service on
operations, the massive
contribution of the erks on the
ground was of immeasureable
value to the RAAF's war
against the Japanese. A typical
scene on most Beau squadrons
or units – any day.

Left: Jungle or no jungle,
ground maintenance had to be
continued. A19-134 (ex-RAF
serial JL854) of 30 Squadron
RAAF undergoing a major
overhaul on December 26th,
1943./*via G Pentland*

Jungle Escapers

A scene which typifies the rugged country over which the RAAF Beaus fought. A8-118, a DAP Mk XXI, of 22 Squadron RAAF following the jungle coastline, searching for Japanese transports or emplacements./*K L Collett*

Above: **A8-85, SK-F, 'HILARY' of 93 Squadron RAAF at Morotai, 1945. It was in this aircraft that Flt Lt V Sims and Fg Off Farrant crashed in the jungle on August 7th, 1945, but evaded capture for three weeks and 'walked back' to their unit.**/*L Blundell*

No matter in which particular campaign of the Far Eastern theatre of operations the Allied airmen fought, all had two common enemies – the Japanese and the jungle. Cruel and implacable as the former was, there was little comparison with the hazards of surviving in the lush hell of a tropical jungle. A combination of swamp and mountain, heat and cold, pest and pestilence, disease and dankness; the jungle represented nature at its cruellest antagonism to any human. To be forced down in it, usually miles behind enemy-held lines, meant almost certain death or, at the very least, grim captivity. Compared with other theatres of war, very few Allied air crews ever 'walked back' from the jungle. Most 'missing' aircraft and their crews were just never seen again – finding death and an unmarked grave in the maw of terrain which seldom gave up its secrets. Those few who did return had to fight raw nature to survive – a meaner opponent than any Japanese foe. Exemplifying the conditions which had to be overcome was one RAAF Beaufighter crew of 93 Squadron who, on almost the last Beau operations of the war were shot down but finally returned to their unit. The pilot's report which follows omits the physical privations and constant psychological effects he and his fellow crew man suffered – these can only be imagined.

The last operational RAAF Beaufighter unit to be formed, 93 (Attack) Squadron – more usually referred to as the '*Green Ghosts*' – came into existence on January 22nd, 1945 in Australia, 93 finally joined No 1 (Mosquito) Squadron to form 86 (Attack) Wing in Labuan, just in time to take part in operations over Borneo. Two Beaus of the squadron's advance party flew the unit's first operational sorties on July 26th but the only sortie mounted by the *Green Ghosts* in any strength took place on August 7th, when eight Beaus, led by the squadron commander Squadron Leader D. K. H. Gulliver in Beau A8-122, attacked Japanese watercraft in the mouth of the Tabuan River, near Kuching. A successful strike resulted in one 800-ton vessel being left sinking, but one Beau was lost over the target area. This was A8-85, piloted by Flight Lieutenant Vernon J. Sims, with his navigator Flying Officer Reg Farrant. Hit by anti-aircraft fire the Beau was finally ditched but the crew managed to evade capture for three weeks before returning safely to their unit. The story of those three weeks in Japanese-held territory is quoted verbatim here from the report eventually submitted by Vern Sims.

'August 7th
On the leg from Labuan to the target, I flew No.2 to the commanding officer. I

saw the CO make his attack and saw his rockets hit the ship, which caused quite an amount of debris to be thrown to a height of 50-100 feet. I commenced my attack about 800 to 1,000 yards behind the CO and after releasing my ripple of rockets, I was forced to break to the right as pieces of the ship were still flying through the air. I then made a steep turn to the left to regain my position as No.2 to the leader. (Later I found out that at this stage my navigator had tried to contact me on the inter-comm to inform me that there was oil pouring from the starboard motor. He was unable to do this however, for as we later learned the VHF had been damaged.) He then left his position and came up through the aircraft to speak to me. All this while I was taking violent evasive action. Fg Off Farrant touched me on the shoulder and pointed to the oil coming from the starboard motor at the same time as I noticed it myself.

I attempted to feather the propeller immediately but could not do so, though I made several attempts. At first it occurred to me to stay low to avoid any ack-ack, but later I decided that the better plan would be to gain height and make for the direction of the sea, in case it should be necessary to ditch. At this stage I was about 800 – 1,000 yards behind the formation and my oil pressure was down to about 10 lb. I decided to keep the power still being given by the starboard motor in an endeavour to gain height. I had full power on the port motor. I also tried the starboard motor with power off and the pitch in full coarse but this made no difference. All the time I was endeavouring to contact the CO and tell him of my plight but could not get through. I did not consider jettisoning fuel or ammunition or placing the IFF switch to emergency. At 200 feet the starboard motor stopped suddenly with a thud, causing much vibration to the aircraft and it became almost uncontrollable in a spiral dive to the right. I pulled both throttles off immediately and got the aircraft back to a straight and level flight but it 'squashed' owing to the lack of power. Before any further action could be taken the aircraft 'squashed' into the jungle. The belly hit the trees and the nose tilted into the heavy and high foliage. The aircraft slipped through the trees and came to rest almost parallel to the ground. I was slightly dazed and remember hearing my navigator enquiring if I was well. As I undid my safety harness, I discovered I was bleeding profusely from the forehead, face and nose, but all bleeding ceased within 30 minutes without first aid.

Great difficulty was experienced in opening the escape hatches as the foliage was still pressing down, and the navigator's cupola had to be smashed before he could get out. I pressed the IFF destruction buttons then. I unstrapped the Tommy gun but was unable to find the emergency rations and first aid kit. This was due to the darkness and the possibility that these articles had been knocked from their normal positions. The starboard motor had begun to burn and smoke, so I jumped from the aircraft and joined Fg Off Farrant who was in a dazed condition and bleeding from lacerations to the head and face, on the ground. We left the scene of the crash immediately and walked through the jungle for half an hour before we paused to take stock of our possessions, and orientate ourselves on the silk map. We concluded as near as possible that we were one mile north-west of KG Bliong, and we had in our possession two enamel water bottles, two Mis-X outfits (E3J), two revolvers and ammunition, a cigarette lighter, two compasses, one Mae West, one tin of flying rations and one flying helmet with goggles, and the time was 1330 hours. One Tommy gun was also taken from the aircraft but this impeded progress and we later buried it.

We walked south through dense jungle until we reached a wide river running east and west, our aim being to reach the Lupar River where we expected to find helpful natives. The terrain became swampy and small deep tributaries blocked our way, so we decided to hide in the centre of very thick undergrowth to formulate our next moves. It was then discovered that Fg Off Farrant had a very nasty wound in his left knee. At 1600 hours we heard jabbering and a party moving towards us. As they approached I could see brown legs through the undergrowth, so we took the precaution of cocking our revolvers. The undergrowth parted and six natives came into view, but they screamed and retreated towards the river. We gave chase, rounded them up and led them back to our hiding place, but none showed any desire to help us. By the use of signs and Malay glossary, and the presents of money we tried to coax them to get a sampan to row us down the river to the coast. The six of them wanted to go and return with a boat at 2100 hours, but we allowed only three to leave and kept the other three as hostages.

These natives told us they had seen the accident, had gone to the crashed aircraft, and then tracked us to our hiding place by the imprint of our Australian-

Above: **ESCAPERS. Flt Lt Vern Sims (left) and Fg Off Farrant being greeted by their 93 Squadron commander, Wg Cdr D K Gulliver after their return from the jungle. Gulliver died on December 10th, 1945 when his Beau, A8-184 hit two RAAF Mustangs on Labuan airstrip and burned out.**/*RAAF Official*

type boots. They said that as far as they knew there had been no Japs near the crash. These fellows indicated the direction of Kuching, but we could not ascertain how far distant it was, nor the name of the river near which we were hiding. They became more friendly, and the youngest of the party kept trying to persuade us to go to their village and meet his father who, he said, could speak English and had in his possession pamphlets dropped by Allied aircraft. But as he also said that he had been working for the Nips at Kuching, we then did not agree. By 2130 hours, as no sampan had appeared, we decided to go with them to the village. We were then led to an open clearing with a raised hut in the centre. They wanted us to sleep in the hut but by this time we had become suspicious and so we returned to our hiding place. Eventually the sampan did arrive but the crew told us to remain hidden as there was a Chinese whom, they claimed, to be bad, in a canoe nearby. The three natives who had stuck with us now left and went off in the boat.

As we now suspected treachery, we moved on, but soon the jungle and darkness barred our way and we sat down to rest. The mosquitoes and the intense cold did not allow us to sleep.

At about two o'clock in the morning we heard an explosion and cannon shots, then we considered these to be from our Beaufighter, so we decided to move on, but progress was extremely difficult. It then became clear that the river would have to be crossed if we wished to make headway. We therefore attempted to swim the river, but after I had swum 15 yards from shore I was caught in a strong current and struggled back only with difficulty. During this attempt my watch, two compasses, cigarette lighter and one Verylite pouch were lost. We then realised that any further progress was impossible so we sat down for the remainder of the night.

August 11th
A stock-take showed that we had four small pieces of chocolate, one tin of

Above: **A8-124, SK-T, 'MARGE', of 93 Squadron RAAF which crashed at Labuan on August 30th, 1945 – the result of its port engine feathering suddenly during landing, causing the Beau to swing violently to starboard.** */E W Robinson*

orange juice and two soup cubes left. No food whatsoever was available from the jungle. Water was still plentiful but we always took precautions to purify it. We were now worried as our strength was failing rapidly, and Farrant's knee was very painful and appeared to be in a bad way with pus pouring from it. We knew that unless we broke through the jungle we would be hard put to live on. We pushed on as hard as we could until 1500 hours. We lit a fire and made hot soup which gave us a new lease of life. We then pushed on again. At 1700 hours we found an abandoned native garden from which we were able to obtain water cress, green bananas and one ripe paw-paw. The going now became much easier. In a position we have since estimated to be about three miles east from Sampun, a part of the jungle had been felled for three-quarters of a mile and 100 yards wide. It looked like a possible abandoned strip site. At about 1800 hours, two miles south-west of Semera, we saw two children who ran away when they saw us, but we followed them to a native house in the middle of a

garden. We were about to approach the house when we saw a Chinese in another garden close by. We made towards the second gardener (we were later told that in the house to which the two children had run, two armed Nips were interrogating the Chinese . . .) The Chinese who we contacted (named Pang Chung) was most helpful in every way and fed us with eggs and rice. He fetched a half-Chinese, half-Dyak named Anthony Bong who spoke a little English. Little success in interpreting from this individual but he went away and returned with a half-Chinese, half-Filipino youth of 17 named Vincent Usurga, who spoke perfect English and was very helpful. Soon many of their Chinese friends arrived, until we were frightened that so many could not keep our secret, but we were assured that they were completely loyal to the English people. Anthony was to obtain a sampan and take us down the creek that night, thence to Labuan, but he returned at midnight without the sampan. So we slept at Pang Chung's house and took turns to remain on guard.

Above: **BEAU AUSSIES.**
Crews of 93 Squadron RAAF
walking past A8-173, SK-Y. L-
R: WO R G Morton; WO R G
Lessels; WO S J Evill; Flt Sgt
M J Paige; and Flt Sgt Norman
Duckmanton./*RAAF Official*

August 8th

Our plans were now to make the coast or procure a boat across the river, so at first light we proceeded northwards. We thought this river to be BG Samaharan. The same difficulties that beset us the evening before caused us to abandon this idea. Soon after we were able to attract the attention of a Malayan boy in a small sampan whom we induced to ferry us across the river. He confirmed our view that this was the BG Samahran. On the opposite shore he gave us some green coconuts, pineapple and some small thin crisp biscuits. We rewarded him with money. We now headed east and half an hour later came to a Chinese house, but the three occupants were reluctant to help us in any way, and when we noticed two children hurrying in the direction in

which we had just come, we thought it was time we pushed on into the jungle. The track was still easterly and we were using the Mis-X compass. The jungle became very swampy; at 1800 hours we stopped for the night under a large tree, but could not sleep because of the mosquitoes, heavy rain and cold, and I had developed prickly heat.

August 9th

Food was now getting low, but we planned to make our stock last six days. Reg Farrant's knee had become very painful, though I had dressed it with sulphinlamide powder. We walked through the jungle, often feet deep in water, stopping to rest 10 minutes in each hour, with a 30-minute break at mid-day. Towards evening we saw a large wild boar which I fired at but missed. We were later able to light a fire but a storm broke at eight o'clock and put an end to this. The night was similar to the two previous and though we hugged together to gain warmth, sleep was impossible.

August 10th
We pushed on very hard today, as we knew we must soon leave the jungle and the swamp if we wished to survive. We diverted north a little but found the ground became even more swampy and the foliage denser. At this stage we estimated we had travelled 10 miles since crossing the river. A fire was impossible due to the damp conditions. No sleep this night. My prickly heat became worse so I gave myself half a tube of morphia. As there was hardly any result I injected the remainder of the tube.

August 12th
After a good breakfast our benefactors hid us in the thick undergrowth and brought us food at intervals. We were to escape with Anthony that night. During the afternoon Vincent informed us that three armed Nips from Simunjan were in a village two miles away, looking for a crashed airman, so we postponed our escape for another night. The story now came to us that there were 10 Japs in the organised search for Allied airmen. In the afternoon an ex-sergeant of the native constabulary, named Natmow, and another constable named Sangtong, came to our hiding place. They informed us that there was a prahu in the river, 14 ft by 4 ft, and they were willing to smuggle us away the next night. This we agreed to. Reg's knee had become stiff and my prickly heat had gone. We slept that night in Pang Chung's house again.

August 13th
At 0530 we were hidden in thick undergrowth. During this day we were visited by many Chinese and their womenfolk, all of whom brought hard-boiled eggs, which we ate for fear of offending them. We were told that after a meeting of the surrounding villagers, called by the Japs this morning, an organised search of the area was to take place the next morning. The whole escape was planned very efficiently and at 1900 hours we walked bare-footed to the boat. We were farewelled with many gifts of food. The idea was for a smaller boat to go ahead, and if this were challenged on the way to the coast as they passed Semera village, we were to turn back. We were hidden in the bottom of the boat covered with grass mats. Before we reached the village Anthony demanded five dollars or he would not go on. We agreed. The first sampan was not challenged but ours was however. The Japs were put off the scent by being told that the boat was proceeding to sea to obtain fish for them. Safely out to sea, we paid five dollars to Natmow who was in the first sampan, then we sailed away alone, setting course for Labuan, but after two hours we hove to and a squall overtook us.

August 14th
We set sail again, travelling about two miles off-shore, and we estimated our position off Rajang R at daylight. Food was plentiful but sleep difficult due to cramp. The crew of our boat comprised Santong, Anthony and a son of a native police sergeant.

August 15th
Cape Mas was identified this day.

August 16th
At daybreak we were 10 miles off Bintulu. At different times during the day we sighted aircraft and although we used our signalling mirrors we were not seen. Progress was slow, for at different times storms and calms caused us to anchor.

August 17th
We ran into very bad weather and the boat was nearly swamped. We were driven ashore which caused us much concern as we knew this to be enemy territory. We made camp in a Sea Dyak's shelter.

August 18th
The heavy seas continued all day and we were unable to launch our boat. We had only rice left for rations and I had contracted sickness in my stomach, and became too weak to raise myself; but I felt better after I had got some warmth from a fire which Santong had lit.

August 19th
At daybreak we were able to set sail and though we hoped to reach Miri we were becalmed and had to heave to. We were now out of fresh water.

August 20th
Still no wind but the boat was rowed and we made Miri at 10.00 hours. We contacted the AIF (9th Division) who admitted us to hospital.

August 21st
Evacuated by Catalina to Labuan.

Belle Beaus

Below: **IN PEACEFUL SKIES. SR914, converted to TT10 standards post-1945, with its target-towing striped livery, showing its paces over the Somerset countryside.**/*Flight International*

Left: **Beau TFX, RD767, with 'thimble' nose radome for its AI Mk VIII radar, and dorsal fin extension. It was later converted to TT10 standards.** /*Bristol Aeroplane Company*

Above left: **TALL TAIL.** R2058, the first Mk II (Merlin-engined) prototype, fitted here temporarily with RR Merlin X engines and having an experimental tall fin/rudder – an effort to counteract a Beau's normal tendency to swing on take-off and landing. It was of three Mk II prototypes, the others being R2061 and R2062. */Bristol Aeroplane Company*

Far left: Flying Officer Ivor Johnsson standing in the cockpit of his Beau VIc, *'MORNING GLORY'*, at RAF Tain, Scotland, on July 29th, 1943. 404 Squadron RCAF. */Public Archives of Canada*

Left: Another 404 Squadron RCAF *'BUFFALO'* – Fg Off Johnny Cummins and his Beau VIc, *'EIGHT BALL'*. RAF Tain, July 29th, 1943. The cartoon figure is a helmeted grasshopper, grasping a Beau control column 'spectacle'. */Public Archives of Canada*

Above right: **SILVER TUG.** NT913, the prototype Mk TT10, seen here at Filton in 1948. */Bristol Aeroplane Company*

Right: **LAST OF THE LINE.** SR919, the ultimate Beaufighter to be produced. It incorporated thimble nose radome, dorsal fin extension, underwing RP rails, and torpedo crutches on its belly. It was later converted to TT10 standards. The last Beaufighter in RAF service – RD761 of RAF Seletar's Station Flight, Singapore, a TT10 – made its final Service flight on May 16th, 1960, piloted by Fg Off H Marshall, who was subsequently presented with the control column handgrip as a souvenir. Thus ended almost 21 years of RAF Beaufighter front-line duties./*Bristol Aeroplane Company*

To the Fallen

A8-95 of the RAAF flying over
the Australian National
Memorial at Victoria – in
tribute to the many hundreds of
Beau crews who never
returned . . ./R Shute

Acknowledgements

In addition to the individual contributors, I am indebted deeply to the following for most generous help, advice and encouragement, listed alphabetically.

S G H Ayscough; M Bailey; C H Barnes; C W Bassett; K Battrick; K L Collett; Rev L W Daffurn, DFC; Air Cmdre R G Dutton, CBE, DSO, DFC; R Field; Norman L R Franks; L G Frise, BSc, FRAeS; K W Goodall; L C Green; T Hellier; W G Herr; W G Hood; J Hopton; N Jones; T D Jordan; Wg Cdr A Judd; Kennedy; M Kerr; W C Kerr; E H Lee; N Malayney; P T Malone; E Malsem; F Martin; G W R Medcalf; K A Merrick; L P Moreton; R A Morris; K Munson; E G Myring, DFC; N W Parnell; G Pentland; H Platt; Grp Capt K W T Pugh, AFC; R G Reed; C Schaedel; A C Schaefer, BEM; C F Shores; J P Small; R Spicer; J W R Taylor; H W Turner; D Vincent; R Leask Ward; H F Watlington, DFM; P H V Wells, DSO; J M Young.

I am equally indebted to Mrs Joan Braham for permission to quote an extract from her husband's book, *Scramble;* and, for 'services above and beyond the call of duty', to Ted Hine of the Imperial War Museum, Peter Robertson and the Photo Staff of the Canadian Public Archives, and Stephen Piercey of *Flight International.* Each displayed a rare patience with my many impositions on their time and goodwill.

Bibliography

Bristol aircraft since 1910, C H Barnes (Putnam, 1964)
Beaufighter, R H H Macaulay (Gale & Polden, 1944)
Air Publication 1721, (Air Ministry, 1940) etc
The RAF in the World War, Vols 1-4, N Macmillan (Harrap, 1942)
Royal Air Force, 1939-45, Vols 1-3, H St G Saunders, (HMSO, 1953)
RAAF Official History, Vols 1-4, (Australian War Memorial, 1954)
RNZAF Official History, Vols 1-3, (Oxford University Press, 1953)
The RCAF Overseas, Vols 1-3, (Oxford Press, 1944-49)
RAAF over Europe, (Eyre & Spottiswoode, 1946)
Desert Air Force, R Owen, (Hutchinson, 1948)
Briefed to Attack, H P Lloyd, (Hodder & Stoughton, 1948)
Winged Phoenix, (HMSO, 1945)
The Defence of the UK, B Collier, (HMSO, 1957)
Fighter Command, P Wykeham, (Putnam, 1960)
The Dangerous Skies, A E Clouston, (Cassell, 1954)
Cover of Darkness, R Chisholm, (Chatto & Windus, 1953)
Night Fighter, C F Rawnsley & R C Wright, (Collins, 1957)
Night Flyer, L Brandon, (Kimber, 1961)
Scramble, J D R Braham, (F Muller, 1961)
Tumult in the Clouds, A Cunningham, (P Davies, 1953)
Task for Coastal Command, H Bolitho, (Hutchinson, 1944)
Two Steps to Tokyo, G Powell, (Oxford UP, 1945)
Profile No.137, P J R Moyes, (Profiles)
Defence until Dawn, L Hunt, 1949
Desert Squadron, V Houart, (Souvenir Press, 1959)
Four, Five, Five, J Lawson, 1951
The Flying Elephants, C Bowyer, (Macdonalds, 1972)
404 Squadron RCAF 25th Anniversary History, (1972)
Fighter Squadrons of the RAF, J D R Rawlings, (Macdonalds, 1969)
Twenty One Squadrons, L Hunt, (Garnstone Press, 1972)
600 Squadron Association Magazine (Various)
Aviation Historical Society of Australia Journal (Various)
Test Pilot at War, H A Taylor, (Ian Allan, 1970)
Aircraft of the RAF since 1918, O Thetford, (Putnam, 1957)